KU-162-220

Contents

Introduction

Imagine that you walked in this morning and the Microsoft Access program was installed on your computer. Your boss wants you to use this database program to create address files, control inventory, or manage information about employees. What would you do?

A few things are certain:

- You need to find your way around Access readily and efficiently.

- You need to identify and learn the procedures necessary to complete a task or accomplish a goal.

- You need a clear-cut, plain-English guide to the basic features of the program.

You need the *10 Minute Guide to Access.*

What Is Microsoft Access?

Microsoft Access is a popular database management system (DBMS). You might think that a database program would be hard to use, but you are in for a nice surprise. Microsoft took the anxiety out of learning and doing database management, by creating an easy-to-use system called Microsoft Access. The program is so easy to use that you can be doing productive work in a few minutes—using your computer to organize, store, retrieve, manipulate, and print information.

With Microsoft Access you can:

- Enter and update your data.

- Quickly find the data you need.

- Organize the data in meaningful ways.

- Create reports, forms, and mailing labels quickly from your data.

- Share data with other Microsoft Windows programs on your system.

The lessons in this book will show you how to use these Access features.

What Is the 10 Minute Guide?

The *10 Minute Guide* series is a new approach to learning computer programs. Instead of trying to cover the entire program, the *10 Minute Guide* teaches you only about the features of Microsoft Access used most often. Each *10 Minute Guide* is organized in lesson format and contains more than 20 short lessons.

No matter what your professional demands, the *10 Minute Guide to Access* will help you find and learn the main features of the program and become productive with it more quickly. You can learn this wonderfully logical and powerful program in a fraction of the time you would normally spend learning a program.

If you haven't yet installed Microsoft Access on your computer, see the inside front cover for instructions.

Conventions Used in This Book

Each of the lessons in this book includes step-by-step instructions for performing a specific task. The following icons will help you identify particular types of information:

Timesaver Tips   These offer shortcuts and hints for using the program effectively.

Plain English   These identify new terms and their definitions.

Panic Button   These appear in places where new users often run into trouble.

Specific conventions in this book help you to easily find your way around Microsoft Access:

What you type	appears in bold, color type.
What you select	appears in color type.
Menu, Field, and Key names	appear with the first letter capitalized.
Selection letters	(letters you press to pull down menus and activate options) are printed in bold type.

Trademarks

All terms mentioned in this book that are known to be trademarks have been appropriately capitalized. Que cannot attest to the accuracy of this information. Use of a term in this book should not be regarded as affecting the validity of any trademark or service mark.

Lesson

Getting Started

In this lesson, you'll learn some basic database concepts, the parts of the startup screen, and how to start and quit Microsoft Access.

An Introduction to Some Database Concepts

Before you start Microsoft Access, you should know some basic concepts. If you are new to working with databases, these definitions will help you:

Database A collection of objects used to manage facts and figures. A database could be used for keeping track of tapes in a video tape library, controlling an inventory, working with a customer list, or keeping a Christmas card list. A database contains one or more tables, as well as other objects (such as reports). An Access database is stored as a single file.

Table An object in a database where facts and figures are stored in a two-dimensional form, in rows and columns.

Field A category of information in a table, such as an address, tape title, or customer ID. Fields represent the columns of a table.

Record A collection of all facts and figures relating to an item in a table. Rows represent the records of a table.

Object   An identifiable unit in a database, such as a table, report, or form.

You can think of a database management system as a filing cabinet. Each database is like a hanging folder in the cabinet, with the various objects (including the tables) as manila folders in the hanging folder.

Starting Microsoft Access

Before using Microsoft Access, you must install it on your computer (see the inside front cover for directions). Once Microsoft Access is installed, you should be able to start it from Windows. Be sure to restart (or reboot) the computer after installing Microsoft Access by using the button on the final installation screen.

First Things First   Before you can install Microsoft Access, you must have Windows 3.1 already installed and started. You must install Microsoft Access from within Windows. If you are not familiar with basic Windows navigation, see the "Windows Primer" in the back of the book for further instructions.

Start Windows by typing WIN at the DOS prompt and pressing Enter. Click the desired group to make it active. For example, if you installed Microsoft Access to the Microsoft Office group, click on the Microsoft Office group to make it active (see Figure 1.1). If the group is not visible, select it from the **Window** menu of Program Manager.

Inactive window   Active window

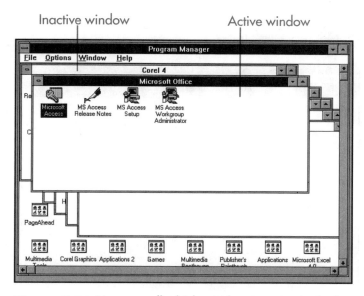

Figure 1.1   You can tell which window is active by looking at the title bars.

Start Microsoft Access either of two ways:

• Double-click the Microsoft Access icon.

• Highlight the icon with the arrow keys and press Enter.

Either way, Microsoft Access starts, displaying the startup window. The menu bar contains two options: File and Help (shown in Figure 1.2). The toolbar contains four active icons: New Database, Open Database, Cue Cards, and Help. From this startup window, you can create or open a database, or you can do basic database management tasks.

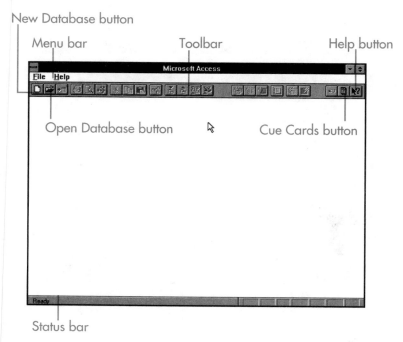

New Database button

Menu bar   Toolbar   Help button

Open Database button   ⬉   Cue Cards button

Status bar

Figure 1.2 The startup screen of Microsoft Access.

Quitting Microsoft Access

To quit Microsoft Access, use one of these methods:

- Select Exit from the **File** menu.
- Press Alt+F4.
- Double-click on the Control-menu box.

In this lesson, you learned some basic database concepts and how to start and quit Microsoft Access. The next lesson shows you the main menu and discusses some of its options.

Lesson

The Startup Main Menu

In this lesson, you will take a brief look at the startup main menu options, learn how the menu bar works, get an introduction to the toolbar, and find out how to get help.

Introduction to the Menu Bar

Microsoft Access uses *dynamic menus*: that is, the options on the menu bar change depending upon how you are using the program. When you first start the program, there are only two options: File and Help. Once you open a database, the menu bar will change and there will be more options.

Selecting Menu Options

Using a mouse is the fastest way to navigate through Microsoft Access. You can practice using the mouse by following these steps:

1. Move the mouse pointer over the desired menu name on the main menu bar and press and release the left button (this is called "clicking"). For example, click File. The menu opens.

2. Click on the desired option in the menu. For example, click Open Database.

3. When the dialog box opens (like the one in Figure 2.1), select the desired options or enter the desired text. (Turn to the Windows Primer in the back of the book for information on working in dialog boxes.)

4. Normally, you close the dialog box by clicking on OK, thereby initiating the action. For this example, click on Cancel to close the dialog box without taking any action.

Click here to close the box and initiate the action.

Click here to close the box and cancel the action.

Figure 2.1   A sample dialog box.

There are a few guidelines to follow when using the menus:

- An item that is grayed on the menu is not available for selection at the current time.

- A small triangle to the right of a menu command means that selecting that command will access another menu. For example, when you have a database open and select the File menu, the **New** command appears on the File menu with a small triangle pointing to the right. Selecting **New** will display a submenu you can use to define the type of object you want to create in the database.

- An ellipsis (three dots) after a command indicates that a dialog box will appear if the command is selected.

- If you open a menu and then decide not to use it, you can clear it from the screen by pressing Esc or by clicking anywhere outside the menu.

Using the Keyboard

The keyboard is used to enter text in a dialog box or database table. In some cases, such as with a laptop computer, you may find the keyboard useful for activating menu commands. Here is how to use the keyboard to issue commands:

1. Press the Alt key and then press the selection letter of the desired menu name.

2. When the drop-down menu is displayed, press the selection letter of the desired option.

Selection Letter   A letter that appears underlined on-screen (bold in this book) and that, when pressed, activates a command from a menu.

I have explained both the keyboard and mouse selection methods in this lesson. However, I will only give mouse instructions in the rest of the book, since using the mouse is usually easier.

Using Shortcut Keys

A number of keys function as shortcuts for certain operations so that you don't have to open the menu and select the command. For example, there are shortcut keys to cancel an operation, cut or copy text, and close the program. Table 2.1 lists a few of the most common shortcut keys.

Table 2.1 Microsoft Access Shortcut Keys.

Key	Function
Alt+F4	Exits Microsoft Access.
Esc	Cancels a menu, command, or dialog box.
F1	Opens the Help system.
Shift+F1	Opens context-sensitive help.
Ctrl+F10	Maximizes the document window.
Ctrl+X	Cuts data to the Clipboard.
Ctrl+C	Copies data to the Clipboard.
Ctrl+V	Pastes data from the Clipboard.
Del	Clears or deletes selected data.
Shift+F2	Zooms in.
Ctrl+F6	Cycles between open windows.
F11	Returns to the database window.
Shift+F12	Saves a database object.

Introduction to the Toolbar

Just under the menu bar is a toolbar with various buttons (icons) that can simplify tasks. Like the menu bar, the toolbars change depending upon the operations you are performing. When you first start Access, the Database Toolbar is on-screen, and there are four active buttons: New Database, Open Database, Cue Cards, and Help. The toolbar is shown in Figure 2.2.

New Database button   Help button

Open Database button   Cue Cards button

Figure 2.2 The Database Toolbar.

Show Me Your Label If you leave the mouse cursor on a toolbar button for a few seconds, a little label will pop up that tells you the button's name.

Getting Help

You can get help at any time by pressing F1, by clicking the Help button at the far right of the toolbar, or by using the Help menu. Choosing Contents from the Help menu will open a Help Table of Contents (shown in Figure 2.3), from which you select any topic you need help with. Double-click the Control-menu box of this window to close the Help window.

Control-menu box

Figure 2.3 The Help window.

If you want to use the toolbar, click on the Help button, and then click on the part of the screen you need help with. For example, if you don't know what the binoculars represent on one of the toolbar buttons, you can click on the Help button and then click on the button in question. A Help screen pops up, telling you that if you click on the binoculars button, you can search for text.

Need Help on a Command? Context-sensitive help is a feature that gives you information on-screen about how to use the menu command that's currently highlighted. To use this help, press Shift+F1 when the command is highlighted (instead of pressing Enter to activate the command).

Another method of getting help is to use the Cue Cards that are a part of Microsoft Access. These electronic tutorials guide you through the various processes, such as creating a database. To use the Cue Cards:

1. Choose the Help menu.

2. Select Cue Cards.

3. Select the option you want help on (such as Build a database with tables if you need help creating a database).

The Cue Cards (shown in Figure 2.4) lie on top of the normal Microsoft Access windows. While you continue working with the program, the Cue Cards guide you.

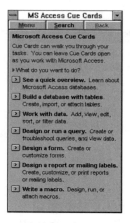

Figure 2.4　Getting help with Cue Cards.

In this lesson, you were introduced to the startup main menu options. You also learned how the menu bar works and how to get help. In the next lesson, we'll create a database.

Lesson

Creating a Database

In this lesson, you will learn how to create a database for tables, reports, and other objects.

Plan Your Database

Suppose you've just been given the task of tracking an important mailing list for your organization: a prospect list for the salespeople. Microsoft Access is a good choice for managing this prospect list because it's easy to use, the salespeople will learn it quickly, and it has all the right features. Let's see how it's done!

Your first step is to define a database. Once that is done, you can decide if tables, reports, forms, and queries are necessary. The prospect list would be a very simple database; a single table and a few reports would probably suffice.

Tables in Databases In this example, the prospects' addresses can be put in a table. The table can then be stored in the same single database file as the reports and forms.

What Are Forms, Queries, and Reports? A *form* is any object you can use to enter, edit, view, or print data records. A *query* is an object used to retrieve specific information from a database based on a condition. A *report* is a collection of information organized and formatted to fit your specifications.

A database can evolve into a fairly complex structure, and it needs to be properly organized. Follow these general rules when you create a database:

- Look at the way the information is currently being managed, and decide if it is the best way.

- Define the new objectives, and build the database to meet these objectives.

- Avoid putting too much information in a single table.

Creating Your Own Database

Let's create a sample database for practice. Remember that you can store tables, queries, reports, and forms associated with the database all in the same database file. To create a new database, follow these steps:

1. Choose New Database from the File menu or click on the New Database button on the toolbar. The New Database dialog box is displayed (see Figure 3.1).

Enter the name of the new database here.

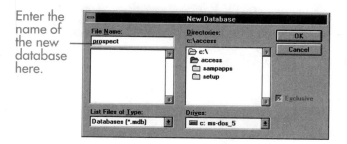

Figure 3.1   Entering the name of the new database.

2. In the File **Name** text box, type the name for your new database. (You can use up to eight characters, plus a three-character extension. If you don't type an extension, Access will automatically add the extension .mdb.) The default name is DB1.MDB, but you can give the file a more specific name. For our example, we'll enter **PROSPECT**.

3. (Optional) If you want to save the database in a different directory, select the desired directory from the **Directories** list box.

4. (Optional) If you want to save the database on a different drive, choose the drive in the **Drives** list box.

5. When you're finished, press Enter or click on OK.

When you have finished creating the database file, a Database window appears on-screen (see Figure 3.2). You can use the displayed window to add tables, reports, and other objects to the database, or you can use any objects you've already created. The list box is empty because you have not yet created any tables, forms, or reports. Notice that you now have more menu options on the menu bar and additional active buttons on the toolbar.

The Database window   The list box is empty.

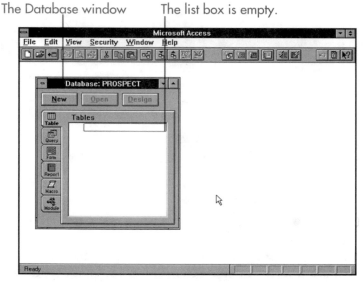

Figure 3.2   The Database window.

What Happened to Those Buttons?   The **D**esign and **O**pen buttons on the new window are dim at this time because no objects have been created in the database yet.

Closing the Database

Closing the database ensures that all objects are properly stored in the database and returns you to the startup window. To close the database, choose Close Database from the File menu. The startup window appears again; if you want, you can open another database or create a new one.

Some Cautions About Closing   By saving the database before you close it, you are ensuring that everything is stored on disk properly. You have to close a database before you can open another one, because only one database can be open at a time in the program.

In this lesson, you learned how to create and close a database. In the next lesson, you will learn how to create a simple table to hold data.

Lesson

Creating a Simple Table

In this lesson, you'll learn how to create a simple table to hold your data.

Designing a Table

First, you need to define the information you want to put in the table. For now, let's look at a database for managing sales prospects. The database will have a single table with the prospects' addresses. What we really need to store now is the name, full address, phone number, a tickle date, a region code, and sales totals for the last six months.

Tickle Date   The *tickle date* is the date when the salesperson should call that prospect again.

Keep It Simple   Keep the database simple. Don't try to put everything you know about the prospect in the file. Decide what data you need to accomplish your purpose, and in what form it should be. Once you have started entering data, you can redefine the database structure as needed for additional data. It's still a good rule, however, to plan ahead as much as possible. It's easier to enter all data for a record at one time than try to add something to each record later.

When you design your table, identify some type of item in the table that will be unique for each record, such as the Social Security number, membership number, or model number for an inventory. Make this unique item the first field in the record; it will be used later as the *primary key*. Access uses the primary key field to *index* your database (see "Setting the Primary Key" later in this lesson). For our example, we'll use the first field to give each person an identification number. The first field will be our primary key field.

What's in a Name?   Don't use a person's name for your primary key field. There could be two people in your database with the same name. Access won't allow two primary key fields to have the same information.

Creating a Table

Now let's create a table for our prospects. If you have already created a database using the steps in the last lesson, use these steps to open that database.

1. Choose Open Database from the File menu, or click the Open Database button on the toolbar.

2. Choose the drive and directory, if necessary, and then choose the database from the File **Name** list.

3. Click on OK or press Enter. The empty database window appears (see Figure 4.1).

Table button   Click here to create
a new table.

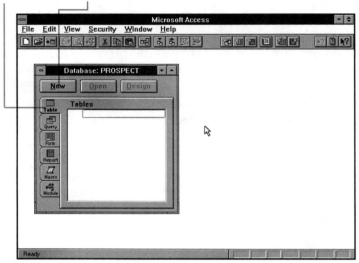

Figure 4.1   The Database window.

Creating a Database   If you have not yet
created a database, create one by choosing **N**ew
Database from the **F**ile menu. To follow along
with this example, type **PROSPECT** in the File
Name text box and choose OK.

Be sure **Tables** is displayed over the list window in the
dialog box. If it is not displayed, click on the Table button at
the left side of the dialog box (see Figure 4.1). To create a
new table, choose the New button. The New Table dialog
box appears. Choose the New Table button to create a
simple table. Microsoft Access opens a new Table window in
Design view (see Figure 4.2). You can use this window to
create the structure of your table.

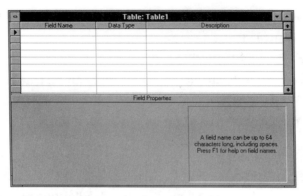

Figure 4.2   Design view for a new table.

> **Design View vs Datasheet View**   Design view is a view of a table, form, query, or report that permits you to modify its basic structure. Datasheet view permits you to view the data of a table, query, or form, but does not allow you to change the structure.

You define a table by telling Access what the structure of the table will be. The structure of a table is made up of *fields*. For each field, you must specify a field name (such as PHONE or LNAME) and a data type (such as Text or Number). You can also enter a simple description if you want. Access supports eight data types:

- **Text** indicates text and numbers that aren't used in calculations.

- **Memo** indicates long text strings (multiple sentences).

- **Date/Time** is used for dates and times.

- **Number** indicates numbers used for calculations.

- **Currency** means that the data is a currency value.
- **Counter** is used for an integer which is incremented automatically.
- **Yes/no** indicates logic values that can be true or false.
- **OLE Object** is used for an embedded object.

For our mailing list, use the following fields:

Field Name	Type	Description
ID	Number	Identification number
LNAME	Text	Last name
FNAME	Text	First name
ADDRESS	Text	Address
CITY	Text	City
ST	Text	State
ZIP	Number	ZIP code
TICKLE	Date/Time	Call-back date
PHONE	Text	Telephone number
REGION	Number	Region
SALES	Currency	Sales for last six months

To create the database structure, follow these instructions:

1. Move the cursor to the first field's text box and enter a field name. (For example, enter ID.)

2. Press Enter or Tab to move to the Data Type column.

3. A default value of **Text** will be entered. If you want to use the Text data type, simply press Enter or Tab to move to the next column. If you want a different data type, click on the down arrow in the Data Type column or press Alt+↓ to open the Data Type list box. For this example, choose Number from the list box.

4. If necessary, go to the last column and type in a description for this field. For this example, type **Identification Number.**

5. Go to the next row and type in the information for the second field. Continue until all fields have been defined.

Setting Field Properties

For each field in a table, you must set certain *properties*. You have already named each field; for now, the only fields for which you need to set properties are the format properties of the ID, ZIP, TICKLE, REGION, and SALES. The text fields do not need to be set in this example.

Property A characteristic of an object, such as its size, color, or name.

To set the properties, follow these steps:

1. To set the ID field format, click on any box in the row that defines the ID field. The Field Properties box at the bottom of the screen will display the current field's properties (see Figure 4.3).

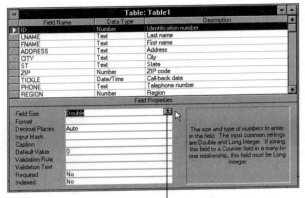

Click here to display a list of property options.

Figure 4.3   The properties of a field.

2. Click on the Field Size box, and an arrow appears. Click on the arrow (or press Alt+↓) to display your options.

3. Choose Long Integer to tell Access you will use whole numbers only.

4. Click on any box in the ZIP row, and change the field size to Long Integer by repeating steps 2 and 3.

5. Click on any box in the REGION row, and change the field size to Integer.

6. To set the TICKLE field format, click on any box in the TICKLE row and click the Format property box.

7. Open the list box and choose Medium Date.

8. To set the SALES format, click on any box in the SALES row and click on the Format property box.

9. If Currency is not the current format, select it from the list box.

Setting the Primary Key

For the next step, you need to set the primary key. The value in this field will be unique for each record, which permits faster access to the record. Microsoft Access does this by creating an index on the primary key field.

Indexing the Database   To organize or sort a table's records according to the content of one or more fields.

To set the primary key, follow these steps:

1. Make sure your table is in Design view. If it isn't, click on the Design View button on the toolbar.

2. Click anywhere in the row of the field you want to use for the index. For this example, click anywhere in the ID row.

3. Click the Primary Key button on the toolbar. A key icon appears in the row selector area to the left of the first field (see Figure 4.4).

Key icon   Primary Key button
  Design View button

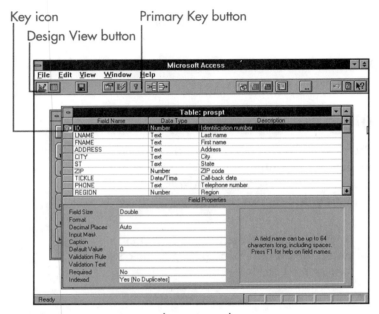

Figure 4.4   Setting the primary key.

Row Selector   The small triangle to the left of the first field of the database is called the row selector. Clicking on any field in a row will move the triangle to that row.

If you save the table without having selected a primary key, Access will ask if you want to create one before it saves the table. If you answer Yes, a new Counter type field is created, and it is used as the primary key field. If you already have a field with the Counter data type, it will be chosen as the primary key field.

Now each time you display the table (as you would when switching from Design to Database view), it will be reordered by the primary key fields (in our example, by ID number).

Saving the Table

Once the table is finished, save it by following these steps:

1. Choose the Save As command from the File menu, or click on the Save button on the toolbar.

2. Enter the name for the table (see Figure 4.5).

3. Choose OK or press Enter.

Figure 4.5   Saving a table.

Closing a Table

To close a table, choose Close from the File menu. If any changes have been made since you last saved the table, Microsoft Access prompts you to save the table. You are returned to the Database window, and the new table is displayed in the list.

In this lesson, you learned how to create a table, set field properties, save the table, and close it. In the next lesson, you will learn how to create a table using the Table Wizard.

Lesson

Using Table Wizard to Create a Table

In this lesson, you will learn how to use the Table Wizard to customize Access' sample tables.

What Is Table Wizard?

Access comes with several *Wizards* to help you create objects like tables, forms, and queries. The Table Wizard helps you create a table quickly by providing you with a list of sample tables. Table Wizard has over 40 sample tables, divided into two categories: Business and Personal. After you choose a category, use a list box to choose the table you want, and then use another list box to select the fields you want.

For example, say you wanted to create a table of all your friends' addresses and birthdays to use as an address list. Using the Table Wizard, you could choose the Friends sample table. A list box will appear, showing all the available field names that are associated with that table. All you have to do is select the field names you want to use, name your table, and set a primary key—and you're done! The formats for each field name are already set, and you don't have to type anything.

Wizards   When you use a Wizard, you are basically just customizing a sample object (like a table or a form). The Wizard will lead you through a series of dialog boxes that ask you questions, allowing you to specify options. Once it has all the information it needs, the Wizard creates the table to your specifications.

Creating a Table

To create a table with Table Wizard, follow these steps:

1. With the Table button selected in the Database window, choose the New button.

2. In the New Table dialog box, select the Table Wizards button. The dialog box shown in Figure 5.1 appears.

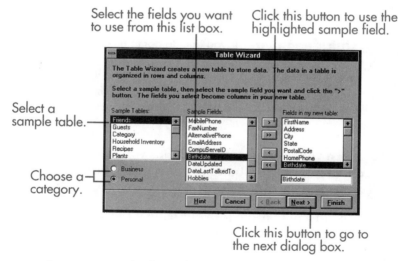

Select the fields you want to use from this list box.

Click this button to use the highlighted sample field.

Select a sample table.

Choose a category.

Click this button to go to the next dialog box.

Figure 5.1   The first Table Wizard dialog box.

3. Choose whether you want to use a table template from the Business or Personal list by selecting the appropriate option button. For example, to create a table for your friends' names and addresses, choose Personal.

4. Select the table you want to use from the Sample Tables list box. For our example, you would choose Friends.

5. Choose each field you want to use in the table by selecting it from the Sample Fields list box. Then click on the > button to move to the Fields in my new table list box.

A Moving Experience Click on the >> button to move all the sample fields to the Fields in my new table list box at once.

Quick Removal If you decide not to use a field name once you've moved it to the Fields in my new table list box, you can easily remove it. Highlight it and click on the < button. Or, click on the << button to remove all the fields at once.

6. When you have selected the fields you want, choose the Next > button. A new dialog box will appear, as shown in Figure 5.2.

7. Type in a new name for your table if the one provided is not what you want.

8. Choose one of the option buttons to tell Access how you want to set the primary key.

9. When you're finished, select the Next > button.

Type a name for your table here.

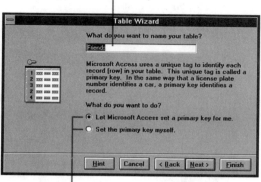

Tell Access how you want to set
the primary key.

Figure 5.2 Customize your table further with the second
Table Wizards dialog box.

10. Depending upon the options you selected, you
might need to answer more questions. If so, more
dialog boxes will appear. Follow the instructions in
the dialog boxes.

11. When you get to the final dialog box (shown in
Figure 5.3), choose an option button to tell Access
what you want to do next.

12. Select the Finish button to have Access create your
table.

This Isn't What I Wanted If you make a
mistake when you're using the Table Wizard,
don't worry. You can edit the finished table in
Design view, just like a regular table.

Displays the table in Design
view so you can edit it.

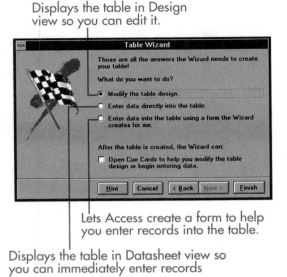

Lets Access create a form to help
you enter records into the table.

Displays the table in Datasheet view so
you can immediately enter records

Figure 5.3 Tell Access what to do next.

In this lesson, you learned how to use the Table Wizard
to customize an existing sample table. In the next lesson,
you'll learn how to add records to your table.

Lesson

Adding Data to a Table

In this lesson, you will learn how to add records to a table and print them.

Opening the Table

In the last three lessons, you created your database and added a table. Now it's time to place your facts and figures into the appropriate fields of the table. Every time you enter a complete row, filling all the fields, you have entered one complete record to the database.

Before you can add records to a table, you must open the database (if it is not already open) and the table. To open a database, choose Open Database from the File menu or click on the Open Database button. Select the desired database and choose OK

> **Quick Return to the Window**   If a database is open, a Database window will be displayed. The title bar shows the name of the database, but the window may be hidden under another window. Use F11 to quickly return to any open Database window.

When you have a database open (such as the one you created in earlier lessons), examine the Database window. Be sure the word **Tables** appears at the top of the list box.

If not, click the Tables button to the left of the list box. The list now displays the current table's objects in the database. Double-click the name of the table you want, or select the desired table (such as PROSPT) and select Open. The table opens, showing empty rows and columns like a spreadsheet (see Figure 6.1). This is called the *Datasheet view*.

Datasheet View A view of a table that displays the data in columns and rows, with the records as rows and the fields as columns. To change to Datasheet view from Design view, just click on the Datasheet View button in the toolbar.

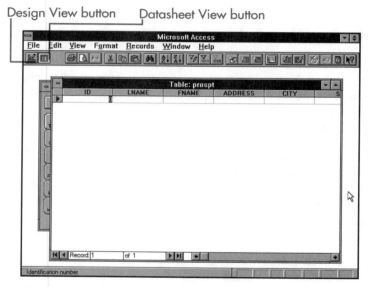

Design View button   Datasheet View button

Figure 6.1 An empty datasheet for adding records.

Adding Records

If you have just created a table, there will be no records in the table. To add a record to the table, fill in the cells for the first row. Use the Tab key, the Enter key, or the arrow keys to move the cursor between the columns as you fill in the data. Pressing Shift+Tab moves you backward through the columns. After completing the entry of a record, you can press the Tab key to move to the first field of the next record and enter that record. Continue until you have added all the records you want to add (see Figure 6.2).

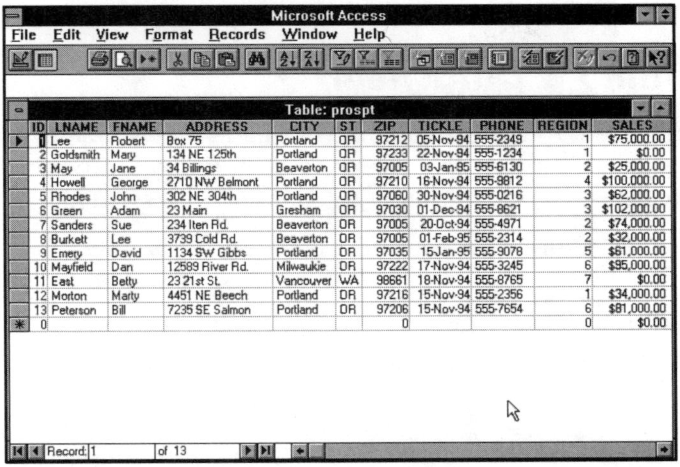

ID	LNAME	FNAME	ADDRESS	CITY	ST	ZIP	TICKLE	PHONE	REGION	SALES
1	Lee	Robert	Box 75	Portland	OR	97212	05-Nov-94	555-2349	1	$75,000.00
2	Goldsmith	Mary	134 NE 125th	Portland	OR	97233	22-Nov-94	555-1234	1	$0.00
3	May	Jane	34 Billings	Beaverton	OR	97005	03-Jan-95	555-6130	2	$25,000.00
4	Howell	George	2710 NW Belmont	Portland	OR	97210	16-Nov-94	555-9812	4	$100,000.00
5	Rhodes	John	302 NE 304th	Portland	OR	97060	30-Nov-94	555-0216	3	$62,000.00
6	Green	Adam	23 Main	Gresham	OR	97030	01-Dec-94	555-8621	3	$102,000.00
7	Sanders	Sue	234 Iten Rd.	Beaverton	OR	97005	20-Oct-94	555-4971	2	$74,000.00
8	Burkett	Lee	3739 Cold Rd.	Beaverton	OR	97005	01-Feb-95	555-2314	2	$32,000.00
9	Emery	David	1134 SW Gibbs	Portland	OR	97035	15-Jan-95	555-9078	5	$61,000.00
10	Mayfield	Dan	12589 River Rd.	Milwaukie	OR	97222	17-Nov-94	555-3245	6	$95,000.00
11	East	Betty	23 21st St.	Vancouver	WA	98661	18-Nov-94	555-8765	7	$0.00
12	Morton	Marty	4451 NE Beech	Portland	OR	97216	15-Nov-94	555-2356	1	$34,000.00
13	Peterson	Bill	7235 SE Salmon	Portland	OR	97206	15-Nov-94	555-7654	6	$81,000.00
0						0			0	$0.00

Figure 6.2 The datasheet after entering a few records.

Adding Records to Existing Records in a Table

If a table already contains records, any records you add will be placed at the end of the table. For example, open the PROSPT table you created in Lesson 3 (if it is not already open). At the end of the table, you will see an asterisk marking a blank or empty record. To add a record, you fill out this row, which in turn opens another record.

In the record selection area to the left of the first field, a right triangle marks the current record. If you start typing a new record without moving to the blank row, you will overwrite the data in the current record. If this happens, you can delete the new data by selecting it and choosing Undo Saved Record from the Edit menu. The new data is deleted, and the old data is restored. Close the table and database when you are finished adding records.

Saving Records

Microsoft Access saves your records to disk as you enter them. Each time you move the cursor to the next record, the program saves the record you just entered (or changed) automatically.

Printing a Datasheet

Sometimes it's easier to look at your datasheet on paper than it is to scroll through it screen-by-screen on your monitor. You can print your datasheet by following these steps:

1. Make sure your datasheet is the active window.

2. Select Print from the File menu.

3. A dialog box appears, showing the options listed in Table 6.1. Select the print options you want.

4. When you're finished selecting options, choose OK. The table is printed.

Table 6.1 The Print Dialog Box Options.

Option	Description
All	Print the entire datasheet.
Selection	Print only the selection you have highlighted.
Pages	Print only certain pages.
From	Use this box to enter the first page to print.
To	Use this box to enter the last page to print.
Print Quality	Enter a number, followed by dpi (dots per inch). A higher number means a better print quality.

Option	Description
Print to File	Check this box to print the datasheet to a file instead of to paper.
Copies	Type the number of copies you want.
Collate Copies	Have pages collated if you select more than one copy.

Print Preview If you want to see what your datasheet will look like before it's printed, select Print Preview from the File menu, or click on the Print Preview button on the toolbar. You can view different pages by clicking on the arrows at the bottom left of the window. To exit Print Preview, press Esc.

The Print dialog box lets you specify *what* you want to print, but you might need to change *how* your datasheet is printed. You do this from the Print Setup dialog box. If you select Setup from the Print dialog box or Print Setup from the File menu, the Print Setup dialog box is displayed. Using this dialog box, you can change any of the options shown in Table 6.2

Table 6.2 The Print Setup Dialog Box Options.

Option	Description
Default Printer	Tell Access to print to the default printer.
Specific Printer	Tell Access to print to the printer of your choice.
Portrait	Print the datasheet across the shorter width of the paper (like a person's portrait).

continues

Table 6.2   Continued

Option	Description
Landscape	Print the datasheet across the longer width of the paper (like a landscape painting).
Size	Select the size of the paper to use.
Source	Specify whether you want to print from the paper tray or from your own paper (manual feed).
Margins	Specify Left, Right, Top, or Bottom margin sizes.
Data Only	Check this box to tell Access to print only the data on the datasheet (no embedded objects).

Can't Print?   Access will display the **P**rint command in the **F**ile menu only if you are in Datasheet view. To change to Datasheet view, select **D**atasheet from the **V**iew menu, or click on the Datasheet View button on the toolbar.

Closing a Table

When you have finished entering data, you should close the table and database. This will ensure that everything is saved to the disk properly and no data is lost. To close the table, follow these steps:

1. Choose Close from the File menu. The table is saved to the disk and is no longer displayed.

2. When you are through with the database itself, close it by choosing Close Database from the File menu.

A Word to the Wise   Although Microsoft Access saves the records automatically as you enter them, a wise computer user will not trust this feature to ensure complete safety. You have no assurance that all your data is on the disk until the database is closed. If you plan to take a break from the computer, close the database; open it again when you return.

In this lesson, you learned how to add some records to a table, save the records, and print them. In the next lesson, you will learn how to edit your records.

Lesson

Editing Records

In this lesson, you will learn how to move around in a datasheet, edit existing records, and move and copy data.

Moving Around in the Datasheet

Once your records are entered, you might discover a few errors that need to be corrected. Fortunately, moving around the datasheet is easy. You can use the shortcut keys in Table 7.1 to move the cursor.

Table 7.1   Moving Around with the Keyboard.

Press	To
Tab	Move the cursor from left to right between fields of a record.
Shift+Tab	Move the cursor from right to left between fields of a record.
Arrow keys	Move up, down, right, or left.
PageUp	Scroll up through the datasheet one screen at a time.
PageDown	Scroll down through a datasheet one screen at a time.
Home	Move the cursor to the beginning of the current record.
End	Move the cursor to the end of the current record.

Press	To
Ctrl+Home	Move the cursor to the first field of the first record.
Ctrl+End	Move the cursor to the last field of the last record.
Ctrl+PageUp	Move left one screen.
Ctrl+PageDown	Move right one screen.

You can also use the mouse to select any field of a record you want to edit: simply click on the desired field. You can click on the arrows in the scroll bars to scroll up, down, left, or right, one row or column at a time. You can also click inside the bar to move one screenful at a time, or drag the scroll box to a new location (see Figure 7.1). When you move the scroll box, the screen moves proportionally.

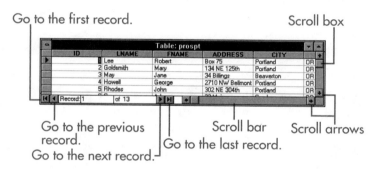

Figure 7.1 Use the scroll bars to move around the datasheet.

Editing Existing Records

To edit a record in a datasheet, first select the field in the datasheet you want to edit. Using the mouse, you can position the cursor anywhere in the field. Or you could use the keyboard to move to the field and do one of two things:

- **Replace the existing data**   If the data in the field is highlighted, you can start typing. The highlighted data is deleted, and the new data replaces it.

- **Keep the existing data**   If the data in the field is highlighted, but you don't want to delete everything, press F2; this lets you move around in the field with the arrow keys. When you're finished, press F2 again.

Deleting Entire Records

If you want to delete an entire record, click on the row selection box to the far left of the record. An arrow appears in the box, and the entire record is highlighted. Select Delete from the Edit menu or press the Delete key. A dialog box appears asking you to confirm your action. Select OK.

Inserting a Record

Since Access sorts the database by the primary key field, new records are inserted in the proper sequence automatically. If you are using sequential numbers as your primary key fields, you have to renumber your records to allow for the new record (if it doesn't go at the end). If you have ten records, for example, and you need to insert a new record as number eight, you change the primary key fields in records eight, nine, and ten. Then you simply type a new record in the bottom row, using the number 8 in the primary key field. When Access saves the table, the records are in numerical order.

Copying and Moving Data in the Datasheet

You can use the Edit menu to simplify your editing by cutting or copying selected material and pasting it. Cutting a selection will move the data from the datasheet to the Clipboard. Copying a selection will keep the data in its original place, as well as placing a copy in the Clipboard. To copy the data from the Clipboard, paste it to your datasheet.

The Clipboard   The data you cut or copy is temporarily stored in an area called the Clipboard. When you paste the data to a new location, the data remains available on the Clipboard for additional pasting until you cut or copy something new to the Clipboard. This allows you to use the **P**aste command repeatedly without having to cut or copy the same data again. When you exit Windows, the contents of the Clipboard are erased.

Cutting Versus Deleting   Cutting a selection is different from deleting it. When you *cut* data, it is deleted from the original location, but a copy of it is saved in the Clipboard for later retrieval. If you *delete* data, it is not placed in the Clipboard and cannot be used for pasting.

Moving Records

Now let's see how the Clipboard works. For example, pretend you have a database exactly like the one in Figure 6.2. After typing the records, you realize that Marty Morton's ID number is actually 13, and Bill Peterson's number is 12. You could move Marty Morton's record by using the Cut command. Here's how:

1. Highlight the data you want to move. In this case, click on the row selection box to the left of the row to highlight Marty Morton's entire record.

2. Open the Edit menu and select Cut.

3. A dialog box appears asking you to confirm your changes. Select OK.

4. To paste the selection to a new location, first position the cursor in the correct row. In this case, move the cursor to the row beneath Bill Peterson's record.

5. Highlight an area that is exactly the same size as your selection. For this example, you would click on the row selection box to select the entire row.

6. Select Paste from the Edit menu.

To make your sample database correct, all you have to do now is change the ID numbers for Marty Morton and Bill Peterson.

Copying Records

Copying selected data is similar to cutting it. The only difference is that the data is not deleted from the original location. For example, seven of the people listed on the datasheet in Figure 6.2 live in Portland; instead of typing the city's name time after time, you can paste copies in each City field. To do this you would:

1. Highlight the data you want to copy. In this case, highlight Portland after the first time you type it.

2. Select Copy from the Edit menu. Access copies **Portland** to the Clipboard.

3. Position the cursor in the correct location. For our example, place the cursor in the City field.

4. Be sure that the area you select to paste the data to is the same size as the area of the data you copied to the Clipboard.

5. Select Paste from the Edit menu.

For our example, you could just select Edit Paste every time you have to enter "Portland"—as long as you don't cut or copy anything else to the Clipboard.

Duplicate Records? If you are copying an entire record to a new location, be sure to change the data in the primary key field. You must have different information in each primary key field so Access can distinguish between records.

Appending Your Selection If you want to paste your cut or copied data to the end of your datasheet, select Paste Append from the Edit menu. This automatically pastes your selection to the last empty record in your datasheet.

In this lesson, you learned how to move around in the datasheet and edit existing records. In the next lesson, you will learn how to edit and rearrange fields in the table structure.

8

Changing the Structure or the View of a Table

In this lesson, you'll learn how to modify a table's structure by deleting, inserting, and rearranging fields.

Changing the Structure of a Table

Changing the structure of a table does not cause any data loss unless you delete a field or change the field properties to a format that doesn't support the existing data.

Safety First! As a safety precaution, always save a database (back it up) before changing a table structure in the database. Do this by copying it to a backup floppy disk.

If you want to change a table's structure, first click on the Design View button on the toolbar to put the table in Design view.

Deleting a Field

You may decide you don't need a particular field anymore and want to delete it from the table. This will save disk space and simplify future data entry.

Fields Versus Records   Don't confuse the terms *field* and *record*. Fields are the pieces of information about each item in your table; they are stored as columns in the table. Records identify all the information about a particular item, and are stored as rows. All the information for Dan Mayfield, for example, might be stored as a single record (row). His address, city, state, ZIP, and telephone number are all fields in that record.

To delete a field, follow these steps:

1. If necessary, open the database using one of these methods:

- Choose Open Database from the File menu.

- Click on the Open Database button in the toolbar.

2. Choose the database file and click on OK.

3. Click on the desired table name and click Design.

Design View button

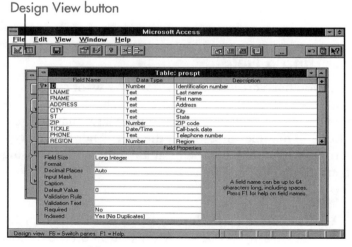

Figure 8.1   Table Design view.

4. Click the row selector for the row that defines the field to delete, or use the arrow keys and press Shift+Spacebar to highlight the row selector (see Figure 8.1).

5. Choose Delete Row from the Edit menu, or press the Del key.

6. Choose OK at the warning prompt.

The field and all the data in it are deleted.

Row Selector   The row selector is the triangle pointer in the space just to the left of the first column in the table.

Be Sure!   Be sure you have selected the correct field. Once you have deleted the field, all data in that field is lost. Data in other fields will not be affected. If you need to recover a deleted field, you must immediately choose Undo Delete from the Edit menu.

Inserting a Field

After you have created a table, you may want to add a new field. For example, after creating a database of a club membership, you may decide to add a field later that defines when the member first joined the club. Microsoft Access permits you to add new fields at any time without losing data in existing fields.

To add a new field:

1. If necessary, switch the display to Design view by clicking on the Design View button on the toolbar, or by choosing Table Design from the View menu (see Figure 8.1).

2. Click on the row selector for the row just below where you want to add the new field (or use the arrow keys to move to the row, and then press Shift+Spacebar).

3. Choose Insert Row from the Edit menu or press the Insert key.

4. Define the new field by entering the field name, data type, and description (see Lesson 4 for more information).

Rearranging the Fields

There may be times when you want to rearrange the fields in a table. You may want to move a primary field (used for an index) so that you can use it as the first field, or (in our example database) you may want to move the phone number field so that it comes before the tickle field.

1. If necessary, switch the display to Design view by clicking on the Design View button on the toolbar, or by choosing Table Design from the View menu.

2. Select the entire row for the field you want to move.

3. Click on the row selector and hold down the left mouse button. Then drag the row. When the row is where you want it to be, release the mouse button.

> **I Made a Mistake**   If you decide the move is not what you want, you can undo the move by immediately choosing Undo Move from the Edit menu.

Changing the View of a Table

Changing the view of the table affects what you see in the Datasheet view, but doesn't change the basic underlying structure. For example, you can make a column smaller, but the structure doesn't change, and any data in the smaller column is not truncated.

Reordering a Field

Sometimes, you might want to change where a field appears in a datasheet without changing its order in the structure. For example, you might want to keep a primary key as the first field in the structure, but give it a more convenient location on the datasheet. To reorder a field position on the datasheet, follow these steps:

1. With the table in Datasheet view, position the pointer on the field selector (the area with the field name above the row). The pointer changes to a downward arrow.

2. Click on the field selector to select the entire field.

3. Click on the field selector, hold down the left mouse button, and drag the column to the new position.

4. To deselect the field, click anywhere else in the datasheet.

Can't Undo You can't undo a reordered field, but the process doesn't destroy any data. If you make a mistake, reorder the fields to return them to the way they were.

Resizing a Field or Column

Resizing a field's column width permits you to tighten up the view, which in turns lets you display more data at a time in the window. To resize the column width for a field, follow these steps:

1. Position the pointer to the right of the column you want to resize, on the line between the field titles. The pointer changes to indicate the border can be moved.

2. Drag the line until the column is the desired size.

You can resize a row in the same way, by dragging the line that separates the rows. Note, however, that resizing one row affects all the rows; they all resize at once.

Save Your Changes

You can use the Save Table command on the File menu to save the new layout. Once you have modified the database structure, choose Close Database from the File menu to save your changes.

In this lesson, you learned how to open a table, and how to delete, insert, rearrange, resize, and reorder fields in the table structure. In the next lesson, you will learn how to create a form.

Lesson

Displaying Tables with Forms

In this lesson, you will learn how to create forms and arrange records in forms.

Forms enable you to enter, edit, and display data a record at a time. If you use Datasheet view to enter records, usually all the fields are not visible at once; you have to scroll constantly as you add, edit, and view records. Using forms, you can see all of the fields of a single record at once. This simplifies data entry.

Microsoft Access includes a Form Wizards button to help you put together forms. This lesson shows you how to use it.

Creating a Form

To create a form, start with the Database window open; click the Form button to select the Forms option. The Database window then lists all of the forms in the database (if it's new, none will be listed). To create a form, follow these steps:

1. Click the New button in the Database window, and you get a New Form window.

2. Open the Select a Table/Query list box to display the tables from which you can build forms. In this example, use PROSPT.

3. Click on the name of the table for which you want to build a form.

4. Choose the Form Wizards button.

5. On the first Form Wizard screen, you are asked to choose an Access Wizard. Choose Single-Column, and then select OK (see Figure 9.1).

Figure 9.1   Choosing the type of form.

6. On the next screen, you are asked to select the fields you want displayed in the form (Figure 9.2). Select the >> button if you want to move all your fields to the Field order on form: box on the right. Click on Next >. Another dialog box appears.

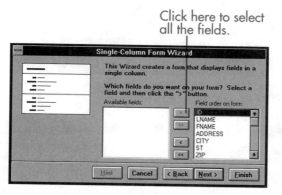

Figure 9.2   Choosing the fields for the form.

7. Figure 9.3 shows the third Form Wizard dialog box. Select a look for the form by choosing Standard, and then click on Next >.

Figure 9.3 Choosing the type of format.

8. On the next screen (shown in Figure 9.4), enter a title for the form and click on Finish. Form Wizard creates the form and displays the table's first record in it (see Figure 9.5).

Figure 9.4 Entering the form's title.

Figure 9.5 The final form.

Viewing Records with a Form

The form you have created can be used to display (view), add, change, delete, or print records. The various objects on the form are known as *controls*.

Controls   On a form or report, a control is an object that displays data from a field, the result of a calculation, a label, graph, picture, or another object.

    Areas of the form that are used for input (for text or numbers) are called *text boxes*. Labels identify each text box, as well as a title for the form. There may also be a *check box* on some forms for entering logical values. (The next lesson shows you other types of controls.)

    To view a particular record, use the Go To command on the Records menu or the navigation buttons at the bottom of the window. To return to a Datasheet view and see multiple records, click on the Datasheet View button on the toolbar or select the Datasheet command on the View menu. Use the Form View button (or select Form from the View menu) to return to the Form view.

Adding Records with a Form

Forms simplify adding records, as all fields of the new record are displayed at the same time. To add a new record with a form displayed, follow these steps:

1. From the Records menu, select Go To.

2. Select New from the list that appears.

3. Enter the data for each field. Press Tab to move the cursor forward between fields; press Shift+Tab to move backward through the fields. Or, you can use the mouse to click on any field.

4. From the last field, press Tab to display an empty form for the next record.

> **Oops!** Select the Undo Current Field command from the Edit menu if you need to restore a field. To restore a previously typed value, choose the Undo Typing command from the Edit menu.

> **Automatic Saving** As you enter or edit records, when you begin a new record, the previous record you entered or edited is saved automatically. You don't need to do anything else to save records as you enter them.

Saving the Form

Once the form design is completed, you should save the form if you intend to use it in the future. To save an open form, follow these steps:

1. Choose Save Form As from the File menu.

2. Enter the name of the form you want to save. (Avoid using the name of any existing table, query, report, or other form.)

3. Choose OK.

Printing Data with a Form

To print data using an open form, follow these steps:

1. Choose Print from the File menu.

2. Choose OK. The data is printed using the form.

Print Preview   If you want to see what your form will look like before you print it, select Print Preview from the File menu or click on the Print Preview button in the toolbar. To exit the Print Preview window, press Esc.

Closing a Form

When you are finished using a form, close it to remove it from the screen. To close a form, choose Close from the File menu. The new form's name will be on the list in the Database window.

In this lesson, you learned how to create a form using Form Wizard, and how to view a record in the form. In the next lesson, you will learn how to customize a form for your specific needs.

Lesson

Creative Form Design

In this lesson, you will learn how to add, resize, and move the labels and text boxes on a form, and how to customize the text.

Modifying a Form Design

After you have created a form with Form Wizard (see Lesson 9), you may want to change the design. Microsoft Access makes this easy: you simply use the mouse to drag and resize.

To start redesigning a form, open your database and click on the Form button in the Database window. The list of the current forms is displayed. Highlight the form you want to modify and choose the Design button. The form opens in Design view (see Figure 10.1).

Notice the differences between this view and a normal form display. The title is now in a separate Form Header area, and an empty Form Footer area has been added. The labels and text boxes are in the Detail area. The toolbar is displayed by default, but you can change your options on the View menu so that the Field List or the Properties List is displayed. A *toolbox* is also displayed.

> **Toolbox** Notice that in Design view, a new window called a *toolbox* is displayed. It contains a special set of buttons that don't appear on the regular toolbar. You use these buttons to design forms. You can move the toolbox by dragging the top title bar, and you can turn it on or off from the View menu.

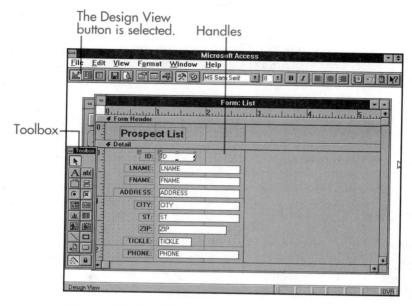

Figure 10.1 A form in Design view.

Resizing Controls

As you learned in Lesson 9, each object on the displayed form is called a *control*. In Design view, you can move and resize these controls and add new controls.

To manipulate a control, you must first select it. You select a text box with a label by clicking on the associated text box. The text box and its associated label are displayed with handles (see Figure 10.1).

- To resize the box vertically, drag the top and/or bottom handles.

- To resize a box horizontally, drag the right and/or left handles.

- To resize a box horizontally and vertically at the same time, drag the corner handles diagonally.

Aligning Your Work   You can use the rulers
to align your work. The rulers should be displayed by default, but if they aren't, you can
select them from the **V**iew menu.

More Than One   You can select more than
one control at a time by holding down the Shift
key as you select.

Moving Controls

Microsoft Access permits you to move a text box and its
associated label together, or you can move each separately.
To move them separately, select the control, and then drag
the large handle in the upper left corner (this is known as
the *move handle*). When you move the text box or label
separately, the mouse pointer will look like a pointing hand.

To move the text box and label together, click on the
control until the pointer looks like a hand with the palm
showing. Now drag the text box and its label to the new
position.

Keep Multiple Selections Aligned   To
maintain the current alignment when moving
multiple controls, select them together, and then
move them.

Adding a Label

A *label* is simply text that is added to the form display
information. The title that's already on the form is one type
of label. You can add additional labels (such as your company name) to the form.

To add a label, use the special toolbox that appears the first time you open a form in Design view. (If it is not already displayed, you can get it by choosing Toolbox from the View menu.) Click on the Label button in the first row of the toolbox. Then click on the appropriate place and enter the text for the label.

Customizing Text

You can modify any text by changing the font, size, color, alignment, and attributes (for example, normal, **bold**, *italic*). To change the appearance of text in a control:

1. Select the control you want to modify. If it contains text, the toolbar will display additional buttons for modifying the text (see Figure 10.1).

2. To change the attributes, click on the Bold button or the Italic button on the toolbar.

3. To change the alignment, click on the Left, Center, or Right buttons on the toolbar.

4. If you want to change the font or font size, you have to set them from the toolbar. To change the font style, click the arrow of the drop-down list box at the middle of the toolbar, and then click on the font. To change the font size, click the drop-down list box to the right of the style box and select the size you want.

After you have completed your work, resize the label to the new text by choosing Size to Fit from the Format menu. Now you can modify the color of the text as needed. To set the color of the text, follow these steps:

1. Click on the Palette button or select Palette from the View menu.

2. From the Palette window (see Figure 10.2), you can set the color of the text or you can set separate colors for fill and outline (simply click on the color of your choice). You can also set the appearance of the text (normal, raised, or sunken) and the border width.

Choose any button.

Click on a color.

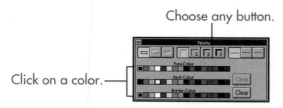

Figure 10.2 The Palette window.

The buttons at the top of the Palette window control the appearance and border type. Leave the mouse pointer momentarily on any button for help on what each button does. (The status line in the main window gives even more information.) The color bars in the work area of the window change the foreground, background, and border colors. Again, you can get a more descriptive title by leaving the mouse pointer momentarily on the bar.

In this lesson, you learned how to move and resize controls, how to add a label to a form, and how to customize your text. In the next lesson, you'll learn how to make a list box on your form.

Creating a List Box on a Form

In this lesson, you'll learn how to add a list box to a form.

Using a List Box

Sometimes it's faster and easier to select a previously defined choice from a list box than to type in text. For example, in the sample database from Lesson 9 (which we'll continue to use in this lesson), all customers live in one of five cities. For the sake of the example, let's assume that all of your future prospects will also live in one of those cities. Rather than type in the name of the city each time (and take the chance of making a typo), you could create a list box that lists those five cities so that you can simply choose a city with one click. Access provides a List Box Wizard to help you create just such a list box.

To create a list box for your CITY field, follow these steps:

1. With the form in Design view, clear an area with sufficient room for the list box. In this example, we will create a list box for the city field, so delete the current city field (select the text box label and press the Delete key).

2. Select each field below the city field (except for the State and ZIP fields) and delete them. (This is just to simplify our work for this example form.)

3. Move the State and ZIP fields down to provide more room for the City list box you will create.

4. Click on the List Box button in the Toolbox (shown in Figure 11.1).

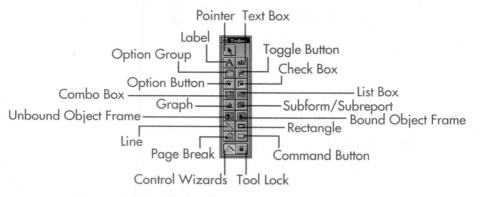

Pointer Text Box
Label
Option Group
Toggle Button
Check Box
Option Button
Combo Box
Graph
List Box
Subform/Subreport
Unbound Object Frame
Bound Object Frame
Line
Rectangle
Page Break
Command Button
Control Wizards Tool Lock

Figure 11.1 The Toolbox.

5. Your mouse pointer will look like a plus sign (+) and will include the List Box icon as you move it into the design area. (Don't hold the mouse button down, just move the mouse.)

6. When the pointer is positioned where you want to put the list box, press the left mouse button and drag the pointer to create the list box. The point at which you start to drag will be one corner of the list box; the ending point will be the opposite corner.

7. A List Box Wizard appears (see Figure 11.2). Click on the option specifying that you will type in the values (the city list) that you want, and then click on Next >.

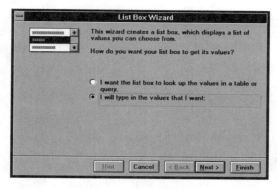

Figure 11.2 Defining the values.

8. In the next List Box Wizard window (see Figure 11.3), set the number of columns to 1 and enter the list of the valid cities you want to choose from. (For this example, type **Portland**, **Beaverton**, **Gresham**, **Vancouver**, and **Milwaukie**.) Then click on **Next >**.

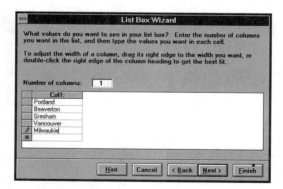

Figure 11.3 Defining the number of columns and the values.

9. On the next List Box Wizard screen (Figure 11.4), click on Store that value in this field:. Click on the arrow to open the list box and select CITY for the field. Click on Next >.

Figure 11.4   Defining the field for the value.

10. In the next window, enter CITY for the list box label and click on Finish.

The new form is now displayed with the new list box. You can edit the form and move controls as necessary.

To see how your new list box looks in the form, click on the Form View button or select Form from the View menu (see Figure 11.5). If the form doesn't look right, you can go back to Design view and change it. If you have scroll bars in your box and don't want them, you can make your list box longer by resizing it in Design view.

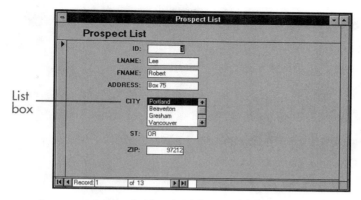

List box

Figure 11.5   The finished form with the list box.

List Versus Combo   Instead of making a list box, you might want to make a *combo box*, so you are not restricted to preset choices. A combo box lets you type a value or choose from a list. To make one, select the Combo Box icon from the Toolbox and follow the steps for making a list box. With a combo box, your choices aren't displayed automatically; you have to select the down arrow button to see them.

Save It!   Be sure to save the form if you want to keep it (choose Save from the File menu). Close the form when you are through using it by choosing Close from the File menu.

In this lesson, you learned how to add a list box to your form. In the next lesson, you will learn how to query your database for more information.

Lesson

Getting Information from a Database

In this lesson, you'll learn how to query a database.

Introduction to Queries

Most of the time you will want to know some specific information when using a database. You won't want to look at the entire database—you just want specific data for making a decision.

The PROSPECT database for sales, for example, might contain hundreds of names, each with its own tickle date (a date that indicates when that person should be contacted again) entered from the previous call. Suppose, as a salesperson, you want only the names that have today's date as the tickle date. To do that, you can build a *query* to access the database and retrieve only the names that meet this criterion. Then you can print a report from the query containing only those names and phone numbers.

What's a Query? A *query* works much like a question directed at a database. In effect, it asks (for example) "Who are the prospects that have today's date as the tickle date?" The query has a *condition* built into it: "What records have a tickle date *equal to* today's date?"

Creating a Query

Let's first create a query for the PROSPECT table. Then we'll modify the query for using it to get today's prospects from the same table using today's date.

1. If the database is not open already, open it so that the Database window is displayed.

2. Click the Query icon. The list window displays any current queries on the database. (In this example, there are none.)

Click on **New.**

Click on **Query.**

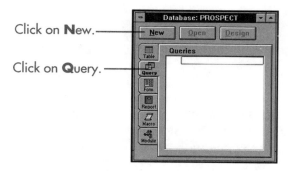

Figure 12.1   The Database window.

3. Click the New button to begin creating a new query.

4. In the next window you can choose to use the Query Wizard or to create a new query. Choose New Query. The Add Table dialog box is displayed (Figure 12.2) with a query grid behind it.

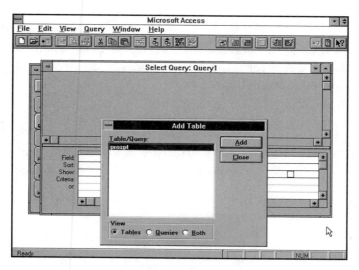

Figure 12.2 Adding the tables.

5. Select the table(s) you want to use for the query. (In this example, select the PROSPT table.) Choose Add. If you are selecting more than one, choose Add after each one.

6. After the last table is selected, choose Close. The fields of the table are displayed in a list box in the Query window. Any field that is used as a primary key appears in boldface.

7. Using the mouse, drag the fields you want to see in the query to the Field row of the QBE grid (see Figure 12.3). Place the fields in the columns in the same order you want them to follow the query. In this example you would drag TICKLE, LNAME, FNAME, PHONE, and REGION one at a time to the Field row.

Datasheet View button

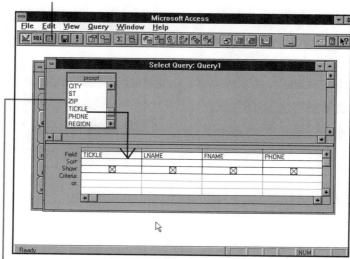

Drag fields into the QBE grid.

Figure 12.3 Drag the selected fields from the field list into the Field row of the QBE grid.

QBE Grid As you create a query, you use a table called a *QBE grid* to define grouping, sort order, and criteria. QBE stands for Query By Example.

Add Fields Fast You can also use the drop-down list in each Field cell to add a field. Click the down arrow, and then click the field name you want to use.

8. Click on the Datasheet View button to see the results of the query. Figure 12.4 shows the result of the query.

Design View button

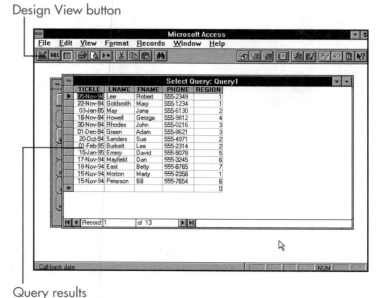

Query results

Figure 12.4 The results of the query.

The results of a query are known as a *dynaset*. Here all the records are displayed because we made no specific query request; no condition was specified.

> **Dynaset**   When you select Datasheet view after you design the query, you will see a dynaset—a dynamic set of records that meet the requirements you asked for in the query. It is considered *dynamic* because the query results change every time you change the data. Each dynaset is temporary—it is not saved. Every time you query a database or change an existing query's design, Access creates a new dynaset.

Now click on the Design View button to return to
Design view or choose Query Design from the View menu.

Selecting Specific Records

Now suppose we want only specific records from the table,
such as those with today's date as the tickle date. To do this,
you must specify criteria.

Criteria Criteria are conditions that a record
must meet to be included in the dynaset. As
Access creates a dynaset, it will include only the
records that meet the criteria you set. In our
example, there is just one criterion: the tickle date.

You can use the Criteria row in the QBE grid to specify
the conditions for record selection. If today's date were
November 15, 1994 and you wanted only records for this
date, you could enter 15-Nov-94 as the criterion in the
column with the field name TICKLE. Notice that after you
press Enter to complete the entry, the date format changes.
Pound signs (#) are added before and after the date. (If you
were doing a text match, as with the LNAME column, quota-
tion marks would appear around the text.)

Now select the Datasheet View button again. Only
those records with the November 15, 1994 tickle date
appear in the dynaset (see Figure 12.5).

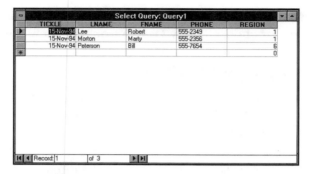

Figure 12.5   The final dynaset.

Specifying Additional Criteria

By adding and combining criteria in the Query window, you can create very powerful queries that meet complex conditions. If you have specified criteria for more than one field (for example, November 15, 1994 for TICKLE and 1 for REGION), a record must meet all the conditions for each field before the query will include it.

You can also specify that you want to retrieve any record that matches one of multiple conditions (an *OR condition*). Assume that you were leaving town for a few days and needed to take with you a list of prospects who would need to be contacted during that time. You could specify as a condition >=15-Nov-94 AND<=17-Nov-94. You could also specify as criteria a list of values using the IN function, as IN(CA,OR,WA) for the ST field. (IN is an operator that permits the entry, in this example, of any one of the values within the parentheses.)

Saving the Query

When you have finished designing your query, save the query by selecting the Save As command from the File menu. In this example, save the query as PROSPQ.

> **Beware of Table Names**   When you save your query, *do not* use the name of any table in the database. If you do, saving the query over-writes the table, and you will lose all your table data. You will get a warning message, but it's easy to ignore the message—especially if you're in a hurry.

In this lesson, you learned how to query a database. In the next lesson, you will learn how to modify and print the queried data.

Lesson

Modifying and Printing Queries

In this lesson, you will learn how to edit tables from a query, modify a query, calculate totals, and print the results of a query.

Editing Tables from a Query

When you run a query on a single table, you can edit the table directly from the displayed query. Display the query in Datasheet view and edit it as you would the original table. (See Lessons 7 and 8 for a review of editing tables.)

> **Can't Edit a Query?** If two or more tables are linked in a query, there may be ambiguity regarding which table contains the data. In that case, Microsoft Access may not let you edit the data in the query (see Lesson 22).

Modifying a Query

Queries can be modified to include new fields, new criteria, or reordered columns. You can modify queries in Query Design view (Figure 13.1). To enter Query Design view, click Query, select the query from the list, and click the Design button.

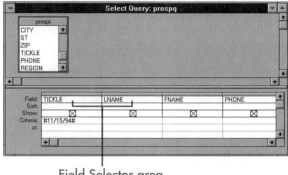

Field Selector area

Figure 13.1   The Query Design screen.

Selecting Columns

To add, delete, or insert columns, you must first select a column to specify where the action is to occur. To select a column, click above the column (in the *field selector*). When you position your mouse in the right spot, the mouse pointer changes to a down arrow. Clicking there highlights the entire column.

> **Field Selector**   The cell area over the top cell of each column. When you click this area, the entire column is highlighted.

Modifying the Criteria

You can modify the criteria at any time by editing the criteria row of the QBE grid. The criteria specifies the condition that must be met for inclusion.

Moving a Column

To move a column in a query, follow these steps:

1. Select the column of the field to move. (You learned to select columns earlier in this lesson.)

2. Drag the column to the new location with your mouse.

Deleting a Column

To delete a column in a query, follow these steps:

1. Select the entire column you want to delete, as you learned earlier.

2. Choose Delete Column from the Edit menu or press Del.

Inserting a Column

To insert a blank column into a query, follow these steps:

1. Select the column to the right of where you want to insert the new column.

2. Choose Insert Column from the Edit menu.

3. Choose a field name from the drop-down list box in the top cell.

Resizing a Column

You may want to resize a column, for example, to get more data on the screen. To resize a column in a dynaset, drag the border of the field selector.

Hiding a Column

There may be times when you want to hide a column in a dynaset. For example, you may want to specify criteria for a field but prefer not to display that field in the Datasheet view. To hide a column, click on the check box on the Show line for that column. An X in the check box indicates that the column will be displayed. The X disappears from the box to show that the column will not be displayed in the dynaset.

Calculating Totals

You can also use a query to show totals. For example, assume the sales to each customer are added to the query, but you only want to see the total sales for each region. You would follow these steps:

1. Add only the fields necessary for the calculations. For our example, you would delete all columns except the REGION and SALES columns.

2. Click on the Totals button in the toolbar, or select Totals from the View menu. A new row called Total appears just below the Field row (see Figure 13.2).

New "Total" row added   Totals button

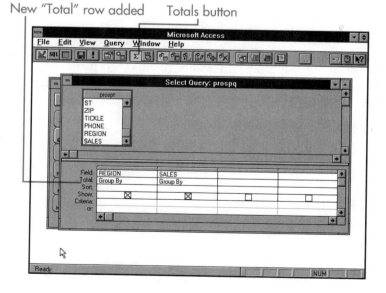

Figure 13.2 The Total row appears below the Field row.

3. Click on the Total row in the column you want to calculate. In our example, you'd click on the Total row in the SALES column.

4. Use the drop-down list box to select the type of calculation you want. In our example, you want the total sales, so you'd select Sum.

5. To see the results of your query, click on the Datasheet View button (Figure 13.3) or select Datasheet from the View menu. In our example's table, the SALES column will show the total sales for each region.

Datasheet View button

Figure 13.3   Click the Datasheet View button to see the query results.

Printing the Dynaset

If your query results are important, it's a good idea to have a printout of your dynaset (the query results). To print the dynaset, be sure the query is in Datasheet view, and then follow these steps:

1. Select Print from the File menu.

2. Select any options desired from the Print dialog box.

3. Choose OK to print.

Print Preview   If you want to see what your dynaset will look like before it is printed, select Print Preview from the File menu, or click on the Print Preview button on the toolbar. You can view different pages by clicking on the arrows at the bottom left of the window. To exit Print Preview, press Esc.

In this lesson, you learned how to modify a query, calculate totals of columns, and print a dynaset. In the next lesson, you will learn how to find data using a form.

Lesson

Finding Data Using Forms

In this lesson, you will learn how to use forms to find specific data in tables, and how to use forms with filters to create data subsets.

Tables, Forms or Queries?

Using tables to find data has limitations. With a table, you can usually see only a few fields at a time. However, forms and queries allow you to get around the size limitations of a table. With a form you can find specific data, create subsets of data, sort data to a specific order, and locate data that meets specific criteria.

Using an Existing Form To follow the instructions in this lesson, you'll need to have a form already created. If you haven't created any forms yet, turn to Lesson 8 and create one now.

Finding Data Using a Form

If you need to find data quickly and you don't want to take the time to build a query, use a form. You can do a simple search to locate the record you need. For example, suppose you need a telephone number for a certain prospect quickly. Let's see how to find it!

To find a value quickly, follow these steps:

1. Open the form if it is not already open. (In the Database window, click the Form button, and then double-click on the form name.)

2. Select the field to search by clicking on the title of the field, or by pressing the Tab key until the field is selected. For our example, you would select the PHONE field.

3. Click on the Find button in the toolbar, or choose Find from the Edit menu.

4. When the Find in field dialog box appears, enter the data you want to find in the Find What text box (see Figure 14.1).

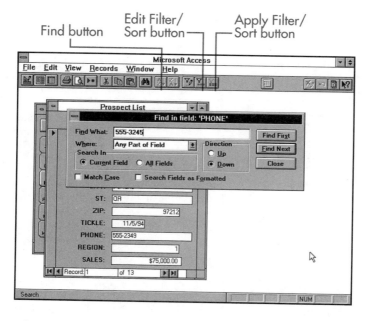

Figure 14.1 Finding data in a record.

5. Select the Where drop-down list and click on an option. Not sure which one you want? They're listed in Table 14.1.

6. Click the Find First button. Access finds the first occurrence of the data you specified.

7. If this is not the record you want, choose the Find Next button to move to the next occurrence.

8. When the search is complete, a dialog box appears, asking if you want to start the search from the top again. Choose No and click the Close button.

Can't See Your Form? If you can't see your form because the dialog box is in the way, move the dialog box by dragging its title bar to a new location.

Table 14.1   Options for the Find in Field Dialog Box.

Option	Description
"Where" lets you choose the location within each field:	
Any Part of Field	Matches the data you specify in every occurrence.
Match Whole Field	Matches only the text you specify.
Start of Field	Finds only the matches that occur at the beginning of a field.
"Search In" lets you specify which fields:	
Current Field	Searches only the highlighted field.
All Fields	Searches every field.

Option	Description
"Direction" specifies how to search the database:	
Up	Searches toward the beginning of the table.
Down	Searches toward the end of the table.
The two remaining check boxes at the bottom set additional options:	
Match Case	Finds only the matches that are in the same case as the data you specify.
Search Fields as Formatted	Finds matches based on how they appear on-screen, not the format they were stored in.

Creating a Filter

You might want to display all the records that contain certain information instead of viewing them one by one with the Find command. Or you might want to specify criteria in more than one field. To accomplish either one, use a filter to create a subset of specific data.

> **Filter** A *filter* uses the data you specify to create a temporary datasheet of records (called a *subset*). A filter can be created only when you are using a form—never from a table or query.

> **Subset** A *subset* is a group of records that contain the data you specified in the filter. A subset is similar to a query's dynaset.

For example, suppose you want to view a subset of the prospects in Region 1 from the PROSPECT database. Follow these steps to create a filter:

1. Open the form if it is not already open.

2. Click on the Edit Filter/Sort button on the toolbar, or choose Edit Filter/Sort from the Records menu. The Filter window opens (see Figure 14.2).

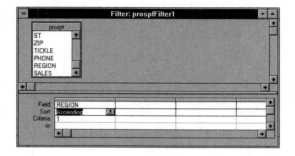

Figure 14.2   The Filter window.

No Calculations Allowed   Notice that you can define the criteria and select the sort order, but you can't perform calculations (as you can in a query).

4. From the field list, drag the desired field to the Field row. For our example, drag the REGION field to the first cell in the first column.

5. Enter the data you want Access to search for in the Criteria row. For example, you would type the number 1 in the Criteria row to tell Access to search for all of the REGION fields that contain the number 1.

6. Open the drop-down list in the Sort row, and select the sort order. In our example, you would choose Ascending so the prospects would be in region order.

7. To see the subset, click on the Apply Filter/Sort button on the toolbar, or choose Apply Filter/Sort from the Records menu.

8. Click on the Datasheet View button to see all the records in the region you selected (see Figure 14.3).

TICKLE:	PHONE:	REGION:	SALES:
15-Nov-94	555-2358	1	$34,000.00
22-Nov-94	555-1234	1	$0.00
15-Nov-94	555-2349	1	$75,000.00
		0	$0.00

Figure 14.3   The results of using a filter.

Don't Panic!   Subsets, much like dynasets, are only temporary datasheets. When you create a filter, you are not changing your data in any way. Access is simply extracting the information you want from your table, and displaying it in a form that's easier to understand.

Saving the Results

Because subsets are temporary, they cannot be saved. However, filters that create subsets can be saved as queries. To save a filter, select Save As Query from the File menu when you are in the Filter window. Name your filter, and then press Enter or click OK.

> **Naming Filters** When saving the filter as a query, don't use the name of any existing table or query or the existing one will be overwritten.

Using a Filter Saved as a Query

After you have saved a filter as a query, you can open it from a form whenever you want. You can also open it as a regular query from the Query list in the Database window. To open a filter from a form, follow these steps:

1. Click on the Edit Filter/Sort button on the toolbar, or select Edit Filter/Sort from the Records menu.

2. Select Load from Query from the File menu. A dialog box appears.

3. Choose the filter you want to use, and click OK or press Enter.

4. Click on the Apply Filter/Sort button on the toolbar, or select Apply Filter/Sort from the Records menu.

In this lesson, you learned how to find data using the Find command and using a filter. In the next lesson, you will learn how to create and use indexes.

Lesson

Indexing Your Data

In this lesson, you will learn how to create single field and multiple field indexes.

Indexes are used to access a specific record in a table quickly. If you have large tables, you will find that using an index speeds up the process of locating records. When you index on a field, the index tells Access where to find the data in the table (as with an index in a book). You can then use the Find command to search within the indexed field for a particular value.

Unlike subsets and dynasets, you cannot see an index. It is not a tool for viewing data, it is simply a way for Access to find your data more quickly. For example, suppose you have a large table that stores records of clients. You search this table often for names of certain people, using the LNAME field. In this situation, using an index would allow you to find the data you need quickly.

Don't Slow Down Indexes are saved along with the table, and are updated automatically when you make changes in the indexed fields. If you need to make many changes to data in an indexed field, remove the index (you'll learn how later in this lesson), update the fields, and then re-index. This is much faster than having Access try to update all of the indexed fields each time you make a change.

To create an index:

1. Click on the Design View button on the toolbar if you are not already in Table Design view.

2. Click on the field you want to index. Its properties will be shown in the window at the bottom of the screen. For our example, you would click on the LNAME field.

3. Click on the Indexed field in the Field Properties box.

4. Use the drop-down list box to select the conditions for your index.

In step 4, you can tell Access not to accept any duplicate values in the field, or you can specify that duplicate values are okay (see Figure 15.1). In our example, you would choose Yes (Duplicates OK) because there might be more than one customer with the same last name.

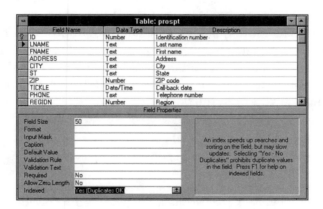

Figure 15.1 Creating an index for a field.

Primary Key Fields When you create a
primary key field (see Lesson 4), Access automatically creates an index on that field and maintains
the index as you update the records in the table.
The index property will be set for Yes (No Duplicates) so
that Access can use the primary key field to distinguish
between the records in the table.

Multiple Field Indexes

If you have a large table, you might search for records using
criteria in two different fields. In that case, you should
consider creating indexes for the two (or more) fields you
search most often.

For example, our sample table from the last section
contains names of our clients. If we have hundreds of
records, chances are good that there are several people who
have the same last name. If you are searching for a client
named Susan Jones, it's easier for Access to find a specific
match if you create an index on the FNAME field as well.

To create a multiple-field index, follow these steps:

1. Click on the Design View button on the toolbar if
you are not already in Table Design view.

2. Choose Indexes from the View menu. A window
appears showing the current indexes.

3. Enter a row for each field in the index, but include
the index name in the first row only (see Figure
15.2). Microsoft Access treats all rows as compo-
nents of the same index until it comes to a row
containing another index name.

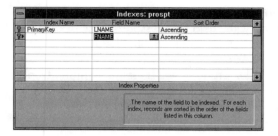

Figure 15.2 Creating a multiple field index.

4. (Optional) If you need to insert a row, click the right mouse button on the row above where you want to insert the new one. Then choose Edit Insert Row.

5. To save changes to the table or indexes, choose Save from the File menu.

Deleting Indexes

You can create as many indexes as you need, but remember that using them will slow down the process of updating your records. You should index only those fields you search often. If you want to delete an index for a field that you don't search often, change the Indexed property to No using the drop-down list in the Field Properties box.

To delete a multiple-field index, select the index in the Indexes window and press Delete.

> **What Am I Deleting?** When you delete an index, you aren't actually deleting any data. Your fields and the data in them remain exactly the same. You are simply telling Access that it doesn't have to remember where your records are for that field any more.

Searching for Records

Once you have created an index, you can use the Find command to search for the data you need. To find a record from a table in Datasheet view, follow these steps:

1. Click on the Find button on the toolbar, or select Find from the Edit menu. The Find in field: dialog box appears.

2. In the Find What text box, enter the data you want to find.

3. Choose any of the options listed for the Find in field: dialog box (for the list, see Table 12.1).

4. Choose Find First. Access finds the first occurrence of the data you specified.

5. If this is not the record you want, choose the Find Next button to move to the next occurrence.

6. When the search is complete, a dialog box appears asking of you want to start the search from the top again. Choose No, and then close the Find in field: dialog box.

In this lesson, you learned how to use indexes. In the next lesson, you will learn how to create reports.

Creating and Using Reports

In this lesson, you will learn how to create a simple report from a table.

Reports are useful for communicating to people in an organized way. With Microsoft Access, the best way to communicate your message is with a form or a report. Lesson 8 showed you how to use forms to communicate your message. In this lesson we'll look at using reports.

Which should you use? Forms are useful for doing simple reporting, as well as for viewing and editing your data. They are limited, however, in that you can't group data to show group and grand totals, you have less control over the layout, and you can't insert a report into a form. Reports can't be used to view or edit data, but allow you to have more layout control, to group data for totals, and to insert another report or graph into a report.

Creating a Report

Microsoft Access includes a Report Wizard feature that makes it easy to create reports from tables or queries. You will use it in this lesson to create a report from a table.

Previewing the Report

The preview mode gives you an idea of what the report will look like and the number of pages that will print before you actually print it. The pages will be magnified, and you can scroll through them using the horizontal and vertical scroll bars. You can use the Page buttons at the bottom of the window to scroll through the pages. The inside arrows move you a page at a time; the outside arrows move you quickly to the first or last page.

To see the entire page, move the cursor to the page (it becomes a small magnifying glass) and click. You can return to the magnified view again by clicking where you want to view.

Preview at Any Time   You can always return to the preview mode of a given report by choosing Print Preview from the File menu.

Printing the Report

You can print the report by choosing the Print button on the toolbar or by choosing Print from the File menu. A Print dialog box appears. Set the options you want and choose OK.

Saving the Report

When you have created the report, you should save it. To save the report, choose Save As from the File menu. Enter the name under which you want to save the report (such as PROSPR) and choose OK. Do not use the name of any existing table, query, or form.

In this lesson, you learned how to create a report. In the next lesson, you will learn how to create custom reports.

Lesson 17

Creating Custom Reports

In this lesson, you will learn how to customize a report form.

Modifying a Report Form

You can modify your report form in various ways. For example, you can move items to other locations, resize them, add labels, and set text attributes. To modify a report, follow these steps:

1. Open the database and choose the Report button in the Database window. The list shows all existing reports in the database.

2. Highlight the report you want to modify and choose the Design button in the Database window. The report is displayed (see Figure 17.1). It can be modified, much like a form.

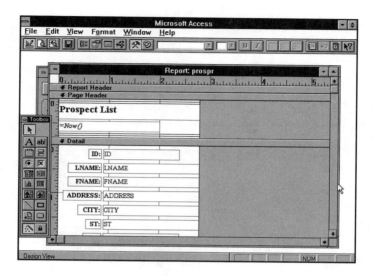

Figure 17.1   The Report Design view.

Resizing Controls

Each object on the displayed report is a control. In the report's Design view, you can move and resize the controls, as well as add new controls.

> **Control**   An object on a report or form that displays the data in a field, a calculation result, specific text, a graph, a picture, or another object.

To manipulate a control, you must first select it. To select a text box with a label, click on the associated text box. The text box and its associated label will be displayed with handles (see Figure 17.2). The handles allow you to change the control in any way you like:

- To resize the box vertically, drag the top or bottom handle.

- To resize a box horizontally, drag the right or left handle.

- To resize a box horizontally and vertically at the same time, drag the corner handles diagonally.

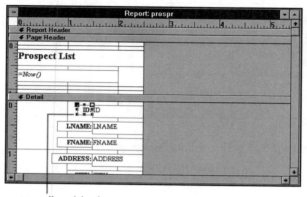

Handles (black squares)

Figure 17.2   Handles surround the selected control.

Use the displayed rulers to align your work. You can select more than one control at a time by holding down the Shift key and clicking on them.

Moving Controls

Microsoft Access permits you to move a text box and its associated label together or separately. To move a text box or label separately, select the control, and then drag the large handle in the upper left corner. This handle is known as the *move handle*.

To move the text box and label together, click on a control. When the pointer becomes a flat-palm hand, drag the text box and its label to the new position.

Use the Rulers   The rulers can help with
alignment when moving and resizing controls.

Adding a Label

A *label* is simply text that is added to the report at a later
time to display information. The title that's already on the
report is one type of label. You can add additional text, such
as your company name, to the report. The label is not bound
to any other control.

To add a label, you use the Toolbox. The Toolbox
appears when you open a report in Design view; if it's not
on-screen, choose Toolbox from the View menu to display it.
Click on the Label button (at the left in the second row; it's
the button with the large A on it). Then click in the report
where you want the label to appear, and enter the text for
the label.

Customizing Text

You can modify any report text by changing the font, size,
color, alignment, and attributes (normal, **bold**, *italic*). To
change the appearance of text in a control, follow these
steps:

1. Click on the control you want to modify.

2. Click on any of the following toolbar buttons to
customize the text:

Button	Function
B	Toggles boldface on or off.
I	Toggles italic on or off.
☰	Sets the text to left alignment.

continues

continued

Button	**Function**
≣	Centers the text in the margins.
≣	Sets the text to right alignment.
Times New Roma ⬦	Selects the desired font.
10 ⬦	Sets the font size.

3. To set the color of the text, click on the Palette button or select Palette from the View menu. From the Palette window (see Figure 17.3) you can set the color of the text, or you can set separate fill and outline colors. You can also set the appearance of the text (normal, raised, sunken) and the border width. Double-click the Palette window's Control-menu box to close the window when you're finished.

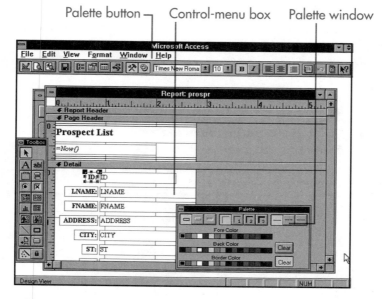

Figure 17.3   The Palette window.

4. After you have completed your work, choose Size to Fit from the Format menu to resize the label to the new text.

> **Toggle?** To *toggle* means to change between two alternating stakes. (A light switch toggles between on and off.)

Adding a Field to a Report

You can add fields to a report form after it is created. Open the report in Design view and then open the field list. You can then drag fields to the appropriate place on the report.

Creating a Report with Grouped Data

You can use Microsoft Access to create reports with grouped data, showing subtotals and totals. For example, suppose you want to create a report showing sales by region with the grand sales total. You would use Report Wizard to create the report from the same table. Use these options for the Report Wizard:

1. Select Report from the Database window.

2. Click the New button in the Database window.

3. In the New Report window, choose the PROSPT table from the list box, and then choose Report Wizards.

4. On the screen that selects the Report Wizard, select Groups/Totals. Choose OK.

5. On the next screen, select the fields to print and their order. Select ID, LNAME, FNAME, REGION, and SALES. Choose Next >.

6. On the next screen, choose to sort by REGION.
Choose Next >.

7. On the next screen, choose to group as Normal.
Choose Next >.

8. On the next screen, set the sort order to SALES.
Click on Next >.

9. Set the look to Executive (the default) and choose
Next >.

10. Enter the title and choose Finish to see the report.

This procedure creates a report with the sales totalled
by region, including a grand total.

In this lesson, you learned how to customize reports. In
the next lesson, you will learn how to create mailing labels.

Lesson

Creating Mailing Labels

In this lesson, you'll learn how to create and print simple mailing labels from your data in the database.

Creating mailing labels is an important part of using address lists effectively. For example, you could print labels from the PROSPT prospect list created in Lesson 5, and use them to mail brochures or letters to the prospects.

Mailing labels come in many sizes and types. Some labels are designed for sprocket-feed printers that pull the labels through. Other labels come in sheets and are designed for laser printers. Labels can also come in single, two, or three-column sheets. Microsoft Access is capable of printing addresses on a wide variety of label types and most common label sizes.

Don't Gum It Up! Use the proper labels for your printer! The adhesive gum used with standard peel-off labels cannot withstand the high temperatures of a laser printer. The labels can come off inside the printer and jam. There are special peel-off labels designed for use in laser printers.

Creating a Mailing Label Report

To make mailing labels, use Report Wizard to create a report in a mailing label format. You can save the report and use it again later.

Let's use the table created in Lesson 5 as an example. If you prefer, you can use any sample database with an address table (such as the Customer table in the NWIND database provided with Access). Follow these steps:

1. If the database is not already open, open it by selecting the Open Database command from the File menu or clicking the Open Database button.

2. When the Database window is displayed, choose the Report button at the left, and then select New. The New Report dialog box appears (see Figure 18.1).

Figure 18.1   The New Report window.

3. Open the drop-down list for the Select A Table/Query box. You'll see the list of available tables and queries.

4. Select the name of the table you want to use for the mailing labels.

5. Click the Report Wizards button.

6. On the first ReportWizard screen, choose Mailing Label and then click on OK (see Figure 18.2).

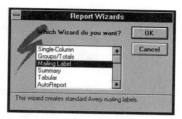

Figure 18.2 Choosing the mailing label report type.

7. In the Available fields list, select the first field you want to include on the mailing label, and then click the right arrow button (>) to move it into the Label appearance box (see Figure 18.3).

Click here to move a field name onto the label.

Punctuation buttons

Figure 18.3 Entering the mailing label design.

8. Use the Punctuation buttons to enter the punctuation desired after the field. For example, you might choose Space between the FNAME and LNAME fields, and then choose NewLine to start the AD-DRESS on the next line.

> **What If I Make a Mistake?** If you make a mistake, click the left arrow button to move an entry back into the left-hand column.

9. Repeat steps 7 and 8 until the entire address appears in the Label appearance box. Then choose Next >.

10. To indicate how the labels should be sorted, select a field name in the Available fields box, and then click the right arrow button (Figure 18.4). For example, you might want to sort by LNAME or ZIP. Then choose Next >.

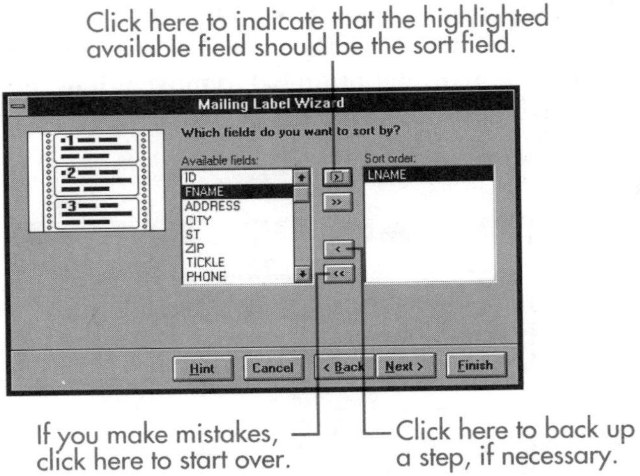

Click here to indicate that the highlighted available field should be the sort field.

If you make mistakes, click here to start over.

Click here to back up a step, if necessary.

Figure 18.4 Choosing the sort order.

11. To choose the size of the mailing label, choose the correct size from the list, and then select Next >.

12. Choose the font and color for the mailing label, and then choose Next >.

13. On the last screen, click on Finish. Report Wizard creates the mailing label report and displays a preview of what will print.

Previewing the Report

The preview mode gives you an idea of what the mailing labels will look like; however, this view of the labels will be magnified. You can use the horizontal and vertical scroll bars to scroll through them. Or you can use the page buttons at the bottom of the window. (The inside arrows move you a "page" at a time; the outside arrows move you quickly to the first or last label.)

To see the entire "page," move the cursor to the page (the cursor becomes a small magnifying glass) and click. You can return to the magnified view again by clicking where you want to view.

You can always return to the preview mode of the mailing label report by clicking the Print Preview button on the toolbar or choosing Print Preview from the File menu.

Printing the Mailing Labels

You can print the labels by following these steps:

1. Choose the Print button on the Print Preview window or choose Print from the File menu. A Print dialog box is displayed.

2. Set the options you want.

3. Choose OK.

Saving the Mailing Label Report

After you have created the mailing label report, you should save it for future use. To save the report, follow these steps:

1. Choose Save As from the File menu.

2. Enter the name you want to use for saving the mailing label report. Do not use the name of any existing table, query, or form.

3. Choose OK.

In this lesson, you learned how to create and print mailing labels. In the next lesson, you will learn how to create graphs.

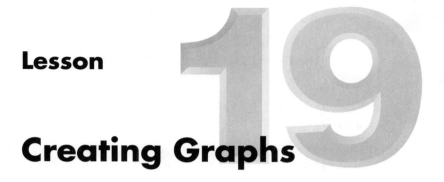

Lesson

Creating Graphs

In this lesson, you will learn how to add a graph to a report.

Introduction to Graphing

Graphs show information in visual relationships and are especially useful for people who don't have time to read an entire report. A busy manager, for example, may find it quicker to look at a graph of sales by region than to decipher a statistical report.

Lesson 5's PROSPECT database shows sales by region, so this lesson will refer to it. (You can use any database, including the Access samples, to try this procedure. In that case, the database, table, and field names will be different.) First, we will create a query on which the report will be based. Then, we will create the report without the graph, using the Report Wizard. Finally, we will add the graph with the Graph Wizard.

Creating the Query

First, let's create the query that shows sales by region. To open the database (if necessary), choose Query and New in the Database window.

1. Choose the New Query button in the New Query dialog box.

2. In the Add Table window, choose PROSPT and click on the Add button.

3. Choose the Close button to close the Add Table window.

4. Scroll to find REGION in the list box. Drag REGION from the list to the first cell of the Field row of the grid.

5. Drag SALES from the list into the Field row of the grid.

6. Click on the Totals button in the toolbar (or select Totals from the View menu) to add a Total row to the grid.

7. The cell under the Field row's SALES cell now contains the words **Group By**. Click on this Group By cell to open a drop-down list box, and choose Sum.

8. Click on the Datasheet View button on the toolbar to verify the totals in a dynaset.

9. Save the query (as SALESQ for this example), using the Save Query As command on the File menu.

10. Press F11 (or close the Query window) to return to the Database window.

Creating the Report

Now that this query has shown us sales by region, use Report Wizard to create a report based on the query.

1. Click on Report and then New in the Database window.

2. In the Select A Table/Query list box in the New Report dialog box, select the query you just created and saved (SALESQ).

3. Choose Report Wizards.

4. Select Single-Column and click OK.

5. On the next screen, choose the field for the report and click the > button to move it to the right column. Or select >> to move both fields to the list box. Then choose Next >.

6. On the next screen, choose the sort order (RE-GION) from the fields, and then select Next >.

7. On the next screen, choose Executive and then Next >.

8. On the next screen, enter a title and choose Finish. When the finished report is shown on-screen, scroll through it and verify that the report totals are correct.

Adding the Graph

Now add the graph to the report by following these steps:

1. Set the report to Design view by clicking on the Close Window button on the toolbar.

2. Scroll down the Report window so that you have 2-3 inches of space under the footer section.

3. Click on the Graph button in the Toolbox (see Figure 19.1). If the Toolbox isn't showing, select Toolbox from the View menu.

Graph button

Figure 19.1   The Graph button in the Toolbox.

4. Using the mouse, drag to draw a control in the area below the report footer section for the graph. Make it about two inches high and six inches wide; use the rulers as necessary. (This will be the size not only of the control, but of the eventual graph.) When you complete the drag, a dialog box will appear (see Figure 19.2).

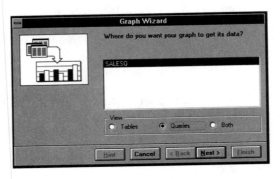

Figure 19.2 The Graph Wizard dialog box.

5. Click on the Queries option button in the View section of the dialog box. Then choose the query on which you want to base the graph (SALESQ), and choose Next >.

6. In the next box, select the field for the graph. Choose SumOfSALES and >, and then select Next >.

7. The next box asks whether to link the graph to the data; choose No. This means the graph won't change if the table's data changes.

8. Choose the Add (sum) the numbers option button, and then click the Finish button.

Choose Print Preview on the File menu to see the report with the graph.

Editing the Graph

If you want to edit the graph, switch to Design view (by clicking on the Design View button). This will open the graph in Microsoft Graph, a modular program that comes with Access (and which resembles the chart mode of Excel, Microsoft's spreadsheet program). You can now add labels or titles and even change the chart type from the menu. To return to Access, choose Exit and Return to Microsoft Access from the File menu.

Printing the Report and Graph

When you are finished creating your report, you should save it (using the Save As command on the File menu). You can then print the report and graph by following these steps:

1. Choose the Print button on the toolbar, or select Print from the File menu.

2. In the Print dialog box, set the options you want.

3. Choose OK.

In this lesson, you learned how to create a graph to use with a report. In the next lesson, you will learn how to use macros to automate your work.

Automating Your Work

In this lesson, you will learn how to automate your work using macros.

After you have used Microsoft Access for a short while, you will probably find there are a few tasks you do repeatedly. For example, you might often find yourself opening a form and going to the end of a table to enter records. Such an action can be automated so that a single command will set up a table for data entry. You can do this with a *macro*.

> **Macro** A series of actions that you program Microsoft Access to perform for you automatically when you enter a specified command.

Creating a Macro

Let's say that you want to create a macro to open a form, open a table, and display an empty form at the end of the table for data entry. Open the database, and then follow these steps:

1. Click on the Macro button in the Database window and choose New.

2. Select Tile from the Window menu so that you can see the Database window and the Macro window at the same time (see Figure 20.1).

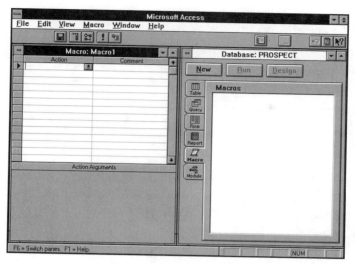

Figure 20.1 Database and Macro windows tiled so you can see both.

Macro Window The Macro window is a two-column sheet in which you enter the actions you want the macro to execute. Many of the actions have *arguments*, which are additional items that you supply to specify how you want the action carried out.

3. Click the Form button on the Database window, and drag the desired form from the Database window to the upper left cell of the Macro sheet. **OpenForm** appears in the cell (see Figure 20.2).

4. Click in the cell directly under **OpenForm** on the Macro window, and then open its drop-down list. Select DoMenuItem.

. . .to this location. When you do, OpenForm appears.

Drag the form . . .

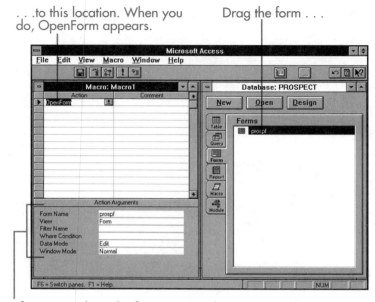

Information about the form appears here.

Figure 20.2   Entering the Action Arguments.

5. In the Action Arguments area, click the Menu Name field (currently containing Edit) and open its drop-down list. Choose Records as the Menu item. In the same way, set Go To as the Command, and New as the Subcommand. Figure 20.3 shows how it should look.

6. Save the Macro window using the Save As command from the File menu. Enter a macro name, such as PROSPM. Click OK.

7. Close the Macro window by double-clicking its Control-menu box or by selecting Close from the File menu. The Database window should still be open.

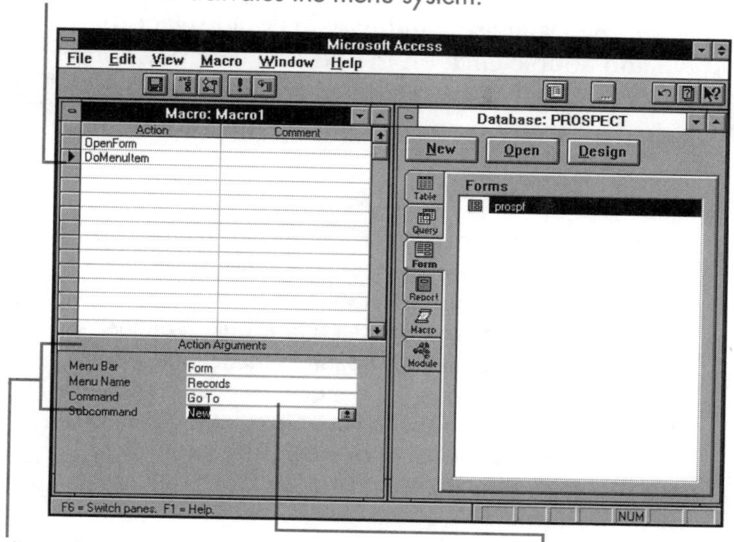

This command activates the menu system.

This information specifies which
menu command to execute.

You can change each
entry by clicking on it and
using its drop-down list.

Figure 20.3   Editing the command arguments.

Executing the Macro

You have now created a macro and saved it. (A macro must
be saved before you can execute it.) To execute the macro
you have just created, follow these steps:

1. Choose Run Macro from the File menu.

2. Select the name of the macro.

3. Choose OK. Access runs the macro. In our example,
it opens the table and form, and then displays the
form positioned after the last record in the table,
ready for a new entry.

There are also other ways of executing a macro. For example, on the Database window you could select the Macro tab and double-click on the desired macro. Another method you can use (when the Macro window is open) is to click on the exclamation point in the Macro window's toolbar.

> **Buttons for Launching Macros**   You can also use buttons to run macros. For example, if you drag a macro name from the Database window to a form, you will see a new button on the form. You can click on this button to launch the macro. With this trick, you can use a macro to open a second form from the first one or to copy data from a previous form entry to the current form entry (such as a city or state).

More with Macros

Once you have had some experience with Microsoft Access, you can create macros for doing much of your routine work (for example, copying data from one form to another). Macros can do it faster—and help ensure that it's done correctly. For more help on macros, see the on-line help system or your documentation.

In this lesson, you learned how to create and use macros in Microsoft Access. In the next lesson, you will learn how to share your data with other programs.

Lesson

21

Using Data with Other Programs

In this lesson, you will learn how to share data between Microsoft Access and other programs you may be using.

Importing, Exporting, and Attaching

You may have already created data files in other programs, such as Microsoft Excel, Lotus 1-2-3, dBASE IV, or Paradox. You can use these data files in Access to build reports, print mailing labels, and do queries. You can also export Access data for use with these other programs.

- When data in an Access database table is converted to a format usable by an *external* program, this is called *exporting* the data. Access keeps the original file intact, and creates a duplicate in a format suitable for the external program's use. The two files are not connected; that is, updating one does not update the other.

> **External Database**   An *external* database is one that is not a part of your open Microsoft Access database. You import data from or export data to an external database.

- When foreign data is converted to Access format for use in Access, you are *importing* the data. Access reads the file and creates a duplicate of it in its own language. Both files remain separate; updating one does not update the other.

- You can also *attach* an external database to a Microsoft Access database. This is slower than importing the data, but it enables you to view, edit, or report from the other program's data as though it were in Access format without actually converting it. In this case, there is only a single file; users of the other program can continue to use it, even while you are updating or reporting from its data in Access.

Exporting Data

When you export data, you are creating a file in the format of another program. Beginning with an open database (such as PROSPECT), let's try an example: exporting a table in the format of dBASE (a Borland database product). Follow these steps:

1. With the Database window active, choose Export from the File menu.

2. In the Data Destination list box of the Export window, choose the destination format—for example, dBASE IV—as shown in Figure 21.1. Choose OK.

Figure 21.1   Starting an export.

3. In the Select Microsoft Access Object window, choose the table name from the list. For example, choose PROSPT.

4. Click the Tables button in the View section at the bottom of the dialog box. Click on OK.

5. In the Export to File dialog box, enter the name of the destination file (see Figure 21.2). Select the drive and directory also, if necessary. Choose OK.

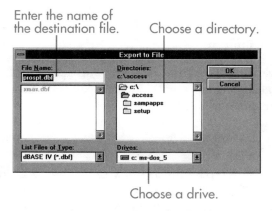

Figure 21.2   Choosing a name for the destination file.

The destination file is created in the desired format. In this case, the file PROSPT.DBF is created.

Importing Data

When you import data, you are creating an Access table from a file in another program's format. This file could be in any of several formats, including Microsoft Excel, Lotus 1-2-3, Paradox, dBASE IV, or an Access file from another database.

As an example, let's see how to import the file we just created. Open a database (such as PROSPECT) if one is not already open. Then follow these steps:

1. With the Database window open, choose Import from the File menu.

2. In the Data Source list box of the Import window, choose the type of input file to import. Choose OK.

3. In the Select File dialog box, choose the drive and directory for the input file and the name of the file you want to import. Select Import.

4. After importing, the screen will display the message "Successfully Imported *xxxx*." Choose OK in the message box. The message will vary with the type of file imported.

5. Click Close to close the Select File dialog box. The Database window will be displayed with the new table name.

Attaching Data

To use an external data file as if it were a table within Access, you can attach an external data file to an Access database. First open the desired database (such as PROSPECT) if it is not already open.

1. Choose Attach Table from the File menu.

2. In the Data Source list box of the Attach window, choose the type of file you want to attach (see Figure 21.3). Select OK.

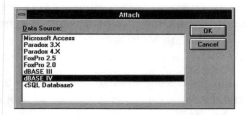

Figure 21.3 Choosing the type of table to be attached.

3. In the Select File dialog box, choose the drive, directory, and name of the file you are attaching. Then click the Attach button.

4. If there is an index file (or files), the Select Index Files dialog box will appear. Select the necessary index file if requested (see Figure 21.4), and choose Select when finished.

5. Choose Close from the Select Index Files dialog box.

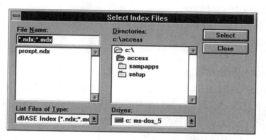

Figure 21.4   The Select Index Files dialog box.

The table is attached to your Access database. You can use it for reports, queries, mailing labels, or graphs as you would any other table.

> **Do I Attach, Export, or Import?**   Using attached tables slows Microsoft Access considerably, but they do make it possible to do your additions, edits, deletions, and reporting from a single file. This makes data control more reliable. Importing and exporting are best suited for moving data permanently between programs, particularly when the data is on different machines.

In this lesson, you learned how to import tables to, export tables from, and attach tables to Microsoft Access. In the next lesson, you will learn how to minimize data duplication by joining tables.

Lesson

Joining Tables

In this lesson, you will learn how to join tables to mini-mize data duplication.

Why Join Tables?

Here's an example of a situation where joining two tables makes sense. In the database example used in the lessons in this book, a REGION code identified the sales area for the prospects. It would be better to identify regions fully with text (such as Vancouver), but all that duplicated text would make the database's main table too large. It saves space to put the region's full identification in a separate table, give each region a code, and use the region codes in the prospect table. Then we can join the two tables in a query and have the query use the region codes to display the text that identifies each prospect. Let's try it!

Create the Table

First create the new table for the regions.

1. Open the database and click the Table button if necessary. Then click the New button.

2. In the dialog box that appears, click on the New Table button. Design view is displayed for a new table.

3. Enter REGION as a field name with a Number format.

4. Enter REGION_NAME as a field with a text format.

5. Select the REGION field, and in the properties for this field, click on Format. Set the Format to General Number.

6. Set the primary key by clicking in the REGION row, and then clicking on the Key button in the toolbar (see Figure 22.1).

Datasheet View button   Key button

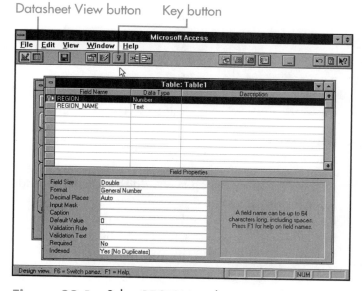

Figure 22.1 Select REGION as the primary key.

7. Save the table as REGIONS (using the Save As command from the File menu).

8. Click on the Datasheet View button to view the datasheet, and then enter the following data:

Under REGION	Under REGION_NAME
1	NE
2	Beaverton
3	Gresham
4	NW
5	SW
6	SE
7	Vancouver

9. Close the table to remove it from the screen.

10. In the Database window, select the Query tab. Choose New. Click on New Query.

11. In the Add Table dialog box, add the REGIONS and PROSPT tables to the query (in that order). The field list of both tables is displayed, with the primary keys in boldface. Choose Close. A line connects the two REGIONS fields in the two tables. This line defines the linkage.

> **No Line?** If the connecting line is not there, you can create it easily. Click on the field in one column, and then drag your mouse over to the field in the other column. When you release the mouse button, a line appears.

12. Drag the desired fields to the Field row. Be sure the REGION and REGION_NAME fields are used (see Figure 22.2). Drag a few more from the PROSPT table.

13. Switch back to Datasheet view by clicking the
Datasheet View button.

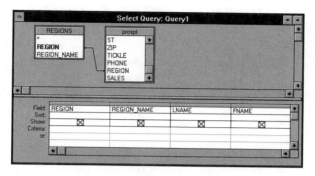

Figure 22.2   Linked tables in a query.

You will see that the link is correct, with each record
showing the correct region name. If you save and close the
query and table now, the link will remain. The next time you
open the query, you will not need to reestablish the link.

> **Link Trouble?**   Links can be a problem when
> you are editing a file from a query. If you need to
> do this and Microsoft Access won't let you, delete
> the link. You can reestablish it after editing.

Deleting a Link

To delete a link in Design view, click on the link to select it.
Then press the Delete key. The linking line disappears, and
the tables are no longer linked.

In this lesson, you learned how to create and delete
links between tables. In the next lesson, you will learn how
to manage your database.

Lesson 23

Managing Your Files

In this lesson, you will learn how to copy, delete, back up, and repair your database files.

What Is Database Management?

Database management is a collection of activities necessary for maintaining your databases effectively and protecting their data. These activities include copying or deleting data as necessary, backing up the system, and repairing damaged databases.

Routine File Activities

First let's look at the routine chores associated with maintaining the databases: copying, deleting, and renaming files.

Microsoft Access stores all the objects of a database in a single file; its file name has an .MDB extension. You can copy, delete, or rename the file from within Windows' File Manager.

First, open File Manager and view the drive and directory that contains your Access Files. Follow these steps:

1. From Windows (Program Manager), double-click the Main program group to open it.

2. Double-click the File Manager icon to open File Manager. It'll look something like Figure 23.1.

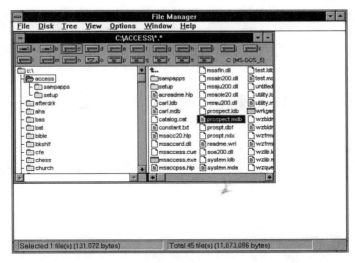

Figure 23.1 Use File Manager for everyday file manipulation.

3. Double-click the drive icon for the drive that contains your Access files.

4. Double-click the directory name on the directory tree for the directory that contains your Access files.

5. Locate the Access file you want to manipulate in the Files window, and click on it once to highlight it.

From here, you can:

- Copy the file by selecting Copy from the File menu and typing the destination in the To text box. Or, to copy to a floppy disk, drag the file onto the drive icon at the top of the window.

- Rename the file by selecting Rename from the File menu and typing a new name in the To text box.

- Delete the file by pressing the Delete key or selecting Delete from the File menu.

Deleting Objects To delete an object (table, report, etc.) from a database, choose the object and then choose Delete from the Edit menu.

Backing Up Your Data

When using Microsoft Access, it's wise to back up your databases frequently. You should always back up a database before making important changes (such as modifying a table structure or making design changes to queries, reports, or forms).

A backup might be nothing more than copying the current database to a file in the same directory using a different name. This can be done quickly from Windows' File Manager.

Back Up Security If you are using user options and security, you should also back up the SYSTEM.MDA file.

In addition to copying key files regularly, the entire system should be backed up periodically, using software designed for this purpose. DOS 6.x comes with MSBACKUP (for DOS) and MWBACKUP (for Windows), two programs that make backing up your entire drive a simple, yet time-consuming, process. Separate backup programs, such as Norton Backup, PC Tools, and Fastback, are also available.

To prevent data loss from fire, flood, or other catastrophe, keep your backup disks somewhere else—at another geographic location. (For example, when you back up data from the office, take the disks home for storage.) Do this on a regular schedule and stick to it, no matter how busy you get. You are most likely to lose data at a time when you are very busy, because it's harder to be careful then.

Repairing Damaged Files

As you use Microsoft Access, keep your databases closed unless you are using them. Anytime the database is open, it can be damaged if there is a power loss or a power surge. You face the same risk if the computer locks up, forcing you to restart your computer.

Microsoft Access will detect previous damage the next time you open the database. If the database is damaged, a message will appear and alert you to the need for repair. Choose the OK button to have Access attempt repair. Once this is done, check the last changes you made and be sure these were completed. You may have to reenter some data or redesign a form or report.

Sometimes a database may be damaged in a way Microsoft Access cannot detect. If you suspect damage, choose Repair Database from the File menu to force repair of the database. If all else fails, copy your backup database files to the hard disk again.

If the Microsoft Access program itself becomes corrupted, it can be installed again from the floppy disks. Just re-run the setup program from Disk 1 (as described on the inside front cover of this book).

Congratulations! You've learned how to use Access to create databases, enter and edit data, build forms, use queries, and create reports. For more information, see the Microsoft Access *Getting Started* and *User's Guide*, or pick up *The Complete Idiot's Guide to Access* by Paul McFedries (Alpha Books, 1994).

Appendix

Microsoft Windows Primer

Microsoft Windows is an interface program that makes your computer easier to use by enabling you to select menu items and pictures so you don't have to type commands. Before you can take advantage of it, however, you must learn some Windows basics.

Starting Microsoft Windows

To start Windows, do the following:

1. At the DOS prompt, type win.

2. Press Enter.

The Windows title screen appears for a few moments, and then you see a screen like the one in Figure A.1.

What If It Didn't Work? You may have to change to the Windows directory before starting Windows; to do so, type **CD \WINDOWS** and press Enter.

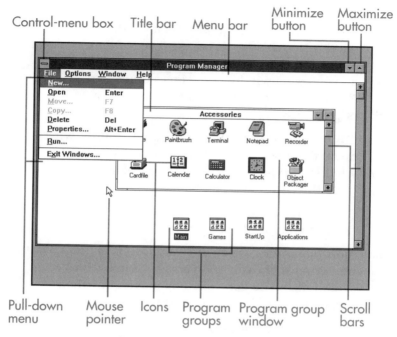

Figure A.1 The Windows Program Manager.

Parts of a Windows Screen

As shown in Figure A.1, the Windows screen contains several unique elements that you won't see in DOS. Here's a brief summary.

- *Title bar*   Shows the name of the window or program.

- *Program group windows*   Contain program icons that allow you to run programs.

- *Icons*   Graphic representations of programs. To run a program, you select its icon.

- *Minimize and Maximize buttons*   Alter a window's size. The Minimize button shrinks the window to the size of an icon. The Maximize button expands the window to fill the screen. When maximized, a window contains a double-arrow *Restore* button, which returns the window to its original size.

- *Control-menu box*   When selected, pulls down a menu that offers size and location controls for the window. Double-click on the Control-menu box to close the currently open window.

- *Pull-down menu bar*   Contains a list of the pull-down menus available in the program.

- *Mouse pointer*   If you are using a mouse, the mouse pointer (usually an arrow) appears on-screen. It can be controlled by moving the mouse (discussed later in this appendix).

- *Scroll bars*   If a window contains more information than it can display, you will see a scroll bar. Clicking on the *scroll arrows* on each end of the scroll bar allows you to scroll slowly. Clicking on the *scroll box* allows you to scroll more quickly.

Using a Mouse

To work most efficiently in Windows, you should use a mouse. You can press mouse buttons and move the mouse in various ways to change the way it acts:

Point means to move the mouse pointer onto the specified item by moving the mouse. The tip of the mouse pointer must be touching the item.

Click on an item means to move the pointer onto the specified item and press the mouse button once. Unless specified otherwise, use the left mouse button.

Double-click on an item means to move the pointer onto the specified item and press and release the left mouse button twice quickly.

Drag means to move the mouse pointer onto the specified item, hold down the mouse button, and move the mouse while holding down the button.

Figure A.2 shows how to use the mouse to perform common Windows activities, including running applications and moving and resizing windows.

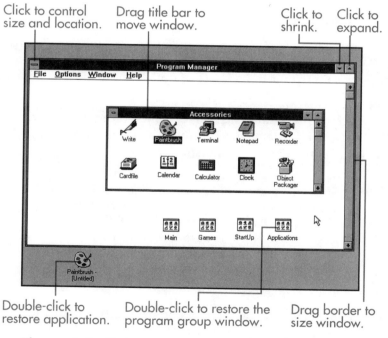

Click to control size and location.　Drag title bar to move window.　Click to shrink.　Click to expand.

Double-click to restore application.　Double-click to restore the program group window.　Drag border to size window.

Figure A.2　Use your mouse to control Windows.

Starting a Program

To start a program, simply select its icon. If its icon is contained in a program group window that's not open at the moment, open the window first. Follow these steps:

1. If necessary, open the program group window that contains the program you want to run. To open a program group window, double-click on its icon.

2. Double-click on the icon for the program you want to run.

Using Menus

The menu bar contains various pull-down menus (see Figure A.3) from which you can select commands. Each Windows program that you run has a set of pull-down menus; Windows itself has a set too.

To open a menu, click on its name on the menu bar. Once a menu is open, you can select a command from it by clicking on the desired command.

Shortcut Keys   Notice that in Figure A.3, some commands are followed by key names such as Enter (for the **O**pen command) or F8 (for the **C**opy command). These are called *shortcut keys*. You can use these keys to perform the commands without even opening the menu.

Usually, when you select a command, the command is performed immediately. However:

• If the command name is gray (instead of black), the command is unavailable at the moment, and you cannot choose it.

- If the command name is followed by an arrow, selecting the command will cause another menu to appear, from which you must select another command.

- If the command name is followed by ellipsis (three dots), selecting it will cause a dialog box to appear. You'll learn about dialog boxes in the next section.

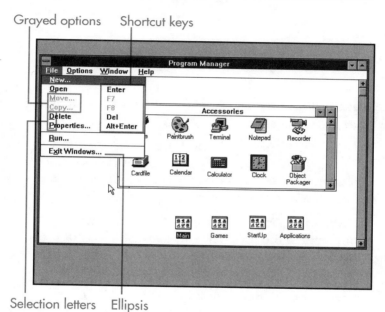

Figure A.3   A pull-down menu lists various commands you can perform.

Navigating Dialog Boxes

A dialog box is Windows' way of requesting additional information. For example, if you choose **Print** from the **File** menu of the Write application, you'll see the dialog box shown in Figure A.4.

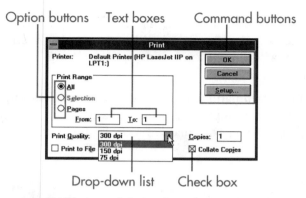

Figure A.4   A typical dialog box.

Each dialog box contains one or more of the following elements:

- *List boxes* display available choices. To activate a list, click inside the list box. If the entire list is not visible, use the scroll bar to view the items in the list. To select an item from the list, click on it.

- *Drop-down lists* are similar to list boxes, but only one item in the list is shown. To see the rest of the items, click on the down arrow to the right of the list box. To select an item from the list, click on it.

- *Text boxes* allow you to type an entry. To activate a text box, click inside it. To edit an existing entry, use the arrow keys to move the cursor and the Del or Backspace keys to delete existing characters. Then type your correction.

- *Check boxes* allow you to select one or more items in a group of options. For example, if you are styling text, you can select Bold and Italic to have the text appear in both bold and italic type. Click on a check box to activate it.

- *Option buttons* are like check boxes, but you can select only one option button in a group. Selecting one button unselects any option that is already selected. Click on an option button to activate it.

- *Command buttons* execute (or cancel) the command once you have made your selections in the dialog box. To press a command button, click on it.

Switching Between Windows

Many times you will have more than one window open at once. Some open windows may be program group windows, while others may be actual programs that are running. To switch among them, you can:

- Pull down the Window menu and choose the window you want to view

  Or

- If a portion of the desired window is visible, click on it.

Controlling a Window

As you learned earlier in this appendix, you can minimize, maximize, and restore windows on your screen. But you can also move them and change their size.

- To move a window, drag its title bar to a different location. (Remember, drag means to hold down the left mouse button while you move the mouse.)

- To resize a window, position the mouse pointer on the border of the window until you see a double-headed arrow; then drag the window border to the desired size.

Copying Your Program Diskettes with File Manager

Before you install any new software, you should make a copy of the original diskettes as a safety precaution. Windows' File Manager makes this process easy.

First, start File Manager by double-clicking on the File Manager icon in the Main program group. Then, for each disk you need to copy, follow these steps:

1. Locate a blank disk of the same type as the original disk and label it to match the original. Make sure the disk you select does not contain any data that you want to keep.

2. Place the original disk in your diskette drive (A or B).

3. Open the Disk menu and select Copy Disk. The Copy Disk dialog box appears.

4. From the Source In list box, select the drive used in step 2.

5. Select the same drive from the **Destination In** list box. (Don't worry, File Manager will tell you to switch disks at the appropriate time.)

6. Select OK. The Confirm Copy Disk dialog box appears.

7. Select Yes to continue.

8. When you are instructed to insert the Source diskette, choose OK since you already did this in step 2. The Copying Disk box appears, and the copy process begins.

9. When you are instructed to insert the target disk, remove the original disk from the drive and insert the blank disk. Then choose OK to continue. The Copying Disk box disappears when the process is complete.

Index

G–H

I